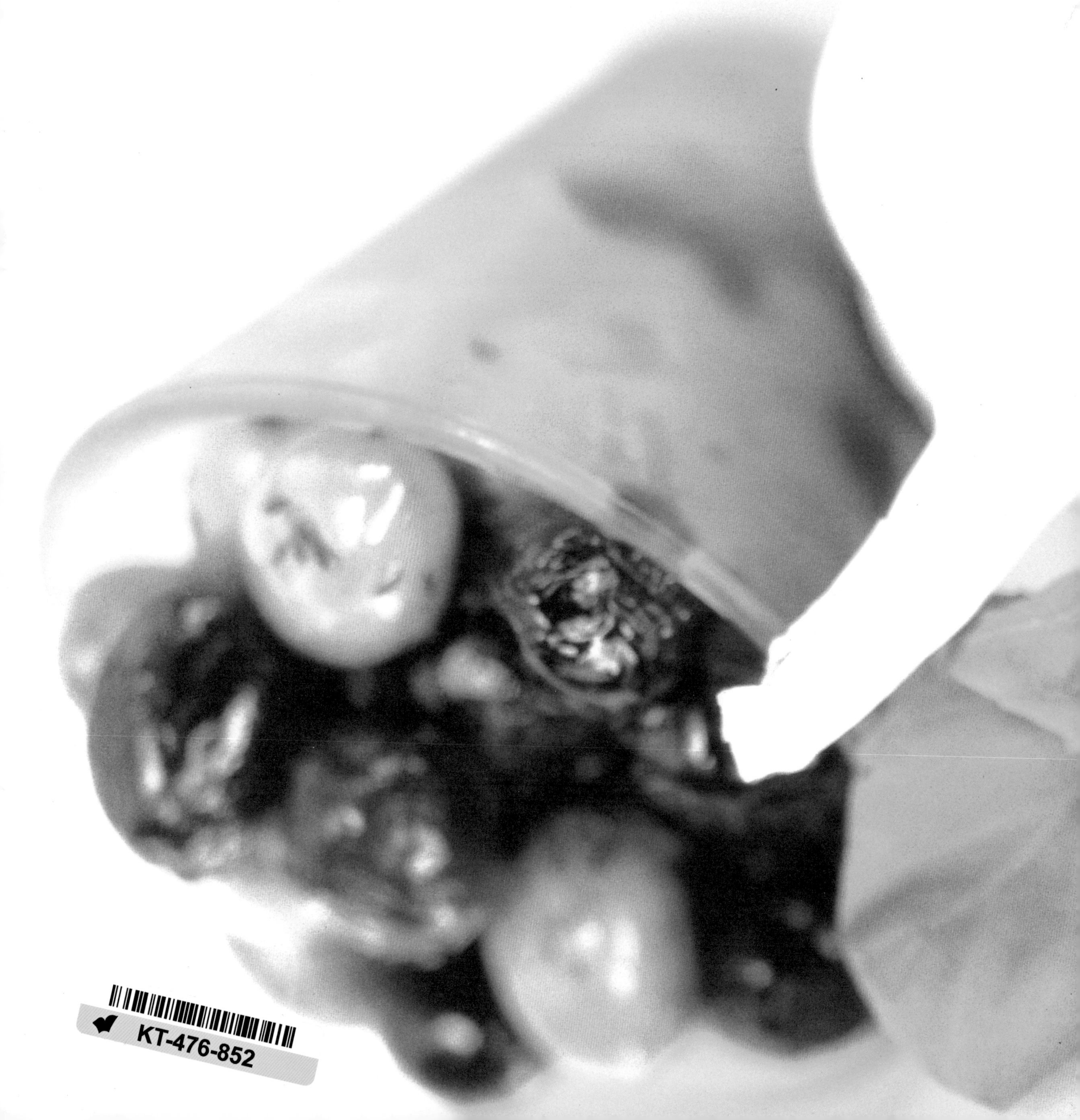

complete

italian

cooking

complete italian cooking

hamlyn

First published in the U.K. in 1997
by Hamlyn an imprint of Octopus Publishing Group Ltd
2–4 Heron Quays
London E14 4JP

Copyright © 1997, 2000 Octopus Publishing Group Ltd

This edition first published in 2000

ISBN 0 600 60189 7

Produced by Toppan
Printed in China

A CIP catalogue record for this book is available from the British
Library

NOTES

Both metric and imperial measurements have been given in all
recipes. Use one set of measurements only, and not a mixture of
both.

Standard level spoon measurements are used in all recipes.
1 tablespoon = one 15 ml spoon
1 teaspoon = one 5 ml spoon

Eggs should be medium to large unless otherwise stated.
The Department of Health advises that eggs should not be
consumed raw. This book contains dishes made with raw or
lightly cooked eggs. It is prudent for more vulnerable people such
as pregnant and nursing mothers, invalids, the elderly, babies and
young children to avoid uncooked or lightly cooked dishes made
with eggs. Once prepared, these dishes should be kept refrigerated
and used promptly.

Meat and poultry should be cooked thoroughly. To test if poultry
is cooked, pierce the flesh through the thickest part with a skewer
or fork — the juices should run clear, never pink or red. Do not
re-freeze poultry that has been frozen previously and thawed.
Do not re-freeze a cooked dish that has been frozen previously.

Milk should be full fat unless otherwise stated.

Vegetarians should look for the 'V' symbol on a cheese to ensure it
is made with vegetarian rennet. There are vegetarian forms of
Parmesan, feta, Cheddar, Cheshire, Red Leicester, dolcelatte and
many goats' cheeses, among others.

Nut and Nut Derivatives
This book includes dishes made with nuts and nut derivatives. It
is advisable for customers with known allergic reactions to nuts
and nut derivatives and those who may be potentially vulnerable
to these allergies, such as pregnant and nursing mothers, invalids,
the elderly, babies and children to avoid dishes made with nuts
and nut oils. It is also prudent to check the labels of pre-prepared
ingredients for the possible inclusion of nut derivatives.

Measurements for canned food have been given as a standard
metric equivalent.

Ovens should be pre-heated to the specified temperature — if
using a fan-assisted oven, follow the manufacturer's instructions
for adjusting the time and the temperature.

Fresh herbs should be used, unless otherwise stated. If
unavailable, use dried herbs as an alternative, but halve the
quantities stated.

Pepper should be freshly ground black pepper unless otherwise
stated.

Contents

Introduction

In Italy, good food and wine are a way of life — an intrinsic part of the Italian character and culture. Meals are important family rituals and consist of several courses. They often last for several hours.

According to its many enthusiastic and loyal devotees, Italian cuisine is second to none. People travel halfway across the continent of Europe not just to gaze at the many artistic splendours that Italy has to offer but also to enjoy the very special authentic home cooking that is on offer at every street corner.

There is plenty of choice available. On the one hand, there are small family tavernas and friendly little pizzerias, and on the other — at the opposite end of the economic scale — there are grand restaurants that can serve you up a veritable banquet. Whatever you want to eat, and however much you have to spend, you are sure to find your heart's desire on a plate.

If you want to be sure of a good meal, follow your nose to the places where the locals eat, whether they be businessmen or lorry drivers. Do this, and you're likely to eat some of the best food in the world.

Variety is the spice of Italian cooking. There is something within the enormous Italian repertoire to suit every taste, every occasion, every age, and every pocket.

The history of Italian food

Italian cuisine has evolved over many centuries. It owes much to many classic European tradition, including Roman, Byzantine and Greek.

Italian food as we know it today, however, derives from the Renaissance, and the many new discoveries and inventions in the arts and sciences. As a result of this exciting new phase in European history, there was also a new interest in food throughout northern and central Italy, in Florence, Milan and Rome. There was a sudden flowering of cookery skills, as the great rulers learned what to do with all the new ingredients that came from the Far East and the New World.

Classic recipes have been handed down over the years through the generations. They are now an established part of family life throughout Italy.

Home cooking

But the best cooking of all in Italy is found in the home. Italian women take enormous pleasure and pride in preparing wonderful dishes for their families — and this is something that you, too, can do.

Of course, you don't even have to travel to Italy to enjoy Italian food. Perhaps the most satisfying way of eating Italian food is to create some of their delicious dishes at home. It is not at all difficult, and your efforts will be well rewarded.

Italian cooking offers a wealth of delicious recipes — some straightforward and some satisfyingly complex, some simple and some more ambitious, some modest and some gloriously flamboyant.

Regional variations

Before Italy was united in 1870 by King Victor Emmanuel II, it was a collection of independent, neighbouring states. These were rarely friendly. On the contrary, they were frequently hostile to one another, which resulted in the people in each state developing a tremendous pride of possession and a sense that everything their state did was better and more special than anywhere else. This applied to everything – their families, traditions, laws, customs, and, of course, food.

Even today, if you travel around Italy from one region to another, you will soon become aware not only of the differences in climate and landscape, but also of the differences in food. There is a wealth of different regional dishes, cheeses and wines throughout Italy. For this reason, it has been said that to get to know Italy is to get to know the world of cookery.

The most noticeable difference is between northern and southern Italy. The north tends to be more industrial and more prosperous than the southern areas, and the northern soil is also more fertile. The south is hotter and the landscape more arid.

As far as cooking is concerned, perhaps the most marked difference is in the different types of pasta. In the north, it is flat, and freshly made with eggs. Tagliatelle, fettucine and lasagne are particularly common in this part of Italy. In the south, on the other hand, tubular, shaped varieties of pasta, such as macaroni, spaghetti, zita, bucatini and rigatoni, are more common.

Arborio rice is grown in the north, in the Po Valley just behind Venice, where it is eaten as a staple ingredient, alongside pasta. Arborio rice is a particularly absorbent type of medium-grain rice and is used to make risottos, such as the well-known Milanese risotto.

In the north, the fat used for cooking is generally butter. In the south, it is olive oil. In the north, delicious cakes and pastries are often eaten, and display a distinctly Germanic influence, as does the game. In the south, the flavours are much stronger, due to a generous use of herbs and spices, especially in the sauces.

The one thing that all the regions of Italy have in common is their joyful approach to food and cooking. There is nothing solemn or self-righteous about food here. Eating is rather one long light-hearted variation on a well-loved theme.

A healthy way

Italian food is not only delicious, it is also one of the healthiest ways of eating in the world. There is no mystery about why this is the case — a quick look at all their staple ingredients soon provides the answer.

Olive oil, fresh vegetables, salads, fresh fish, seafood, pasta, rice: these are all mouthwatering foods, but they are also very good for you. Full of vitamins and minerals, they are also blissfully low in saturated fat.

It is no surprise, then, that Italian cooking is particularly beneficial to a healthy heart. It is also no coincidence that the Italians have such a gratifyingly low incidence of heart disease.

Their way of eating, which is now acknowledged to be one of the healthiest diets in the world, clearly pays rich dividends. It therefore makes good sense to incorporate these ingredients into our day-to-day cooking.

Ingredients

The Italians are fortunate in having such a splendid cornucopia of marvellous ingredients at their disposal. Italian women love to go out shopping in the colourful street markets and grocery stores where they regularly stock up on all their preferred ingredients. With these on hand they are always ready to make their favourite — and their family's favourite — dishes.

Perhaps most important of all, the Italians treat their ingredients with great respect. There are no random choices in the way they shop or cook. They select their ingredients carefully, they store them wisely, and they use them judiciously.

Essential storecupboard ingredients for cooking the Italian way are simple. The most important ingredient of all is probably olive oil, and it's best to invest in a light one for cooking and a heavier, fuller-flavoured one for making salads. Details of typical ingredients are given in special features throughout the book.

Storecupboard essentials

If you want to cook Italian dishes, it is useful to keep a stock of the following non-perishable items in your storecupboard, as they will all come in useful.
• Pasta is perhaps what people think of first when they think of Italian food. It is available both fresh and dried. A lot of people prefer the fresh kind, but even if this applies to you a stock of dried pasta is essential to cope with all emergencies. Pasta is made with durum wheat flour bound with eggs, oil or both. Sometimes it is coloured with spinach or beetroot. It is a good idea to keep a range of different pastas in the cupboard, including a few of the less common shapes. The small varieties are useful for adding to soups.
• Rice is the other main staple food in Italy, along with pasta. Italian Arborio rice is a thick, stubby variety, which absorbs more liquid than other types of rice and is particularly good for making creamy risottos.
• Canned tomatoes are an absolute must in Italian cooking. Canned Italian plum tomatoes are full of flavour, as well as being an excellent convenience food. They are even better than fresh English or Dutch tomatoes, which tend to be low in flavour, and are much easier to use. They always come peeled, and they sometimes come ready-chopped, which makes them even easier to use.
• Tomato purée adds flavour and colour to any dish in which fresh or canned tomatoes are used.
• Olives are frequently used in Italian cooking. As well as useful ingredients in antipasti, they are also used in sauces and casserole dishes. Keep a stock of green, black and stuffed olives in bottles or plastic packs, and buy fresh loose ones whenever possible as these are the best.
• Capers are another excellent standby, which add flavour and authenticity to various fish dishes. They also add zest to certain sauces, as well as being a useful garnish.
• Antipasti are available in jars from many supermarkets and are a useful standby for including in many dishes. They include sun-dried tomatoes (delicious chopped up and used in pasta sauces), artichoke hearts, wild mushrooms and marinated peppers.
• Pesto, made with basil, Parmesan cheese and olive oil, is best made fresh, but the varieties available in jars are a very acceptable alternative. Red pesto has sun-dried tomatoes added to it. You can use it on pasta, or incorporate it into a pasta sauce.

Pasta

Devotees are convinced that fresh pasta is far superior to the dried kind. Fortunately, fresh pasta is easy to make at home, with or without a pasta machine. A machine is simple to use and will give you a more uniform result, but it is perfectly possible to make excellent pasta dough without a machine and to cut the dough by hand. Whatever method you use, it is well worth the effort, because the end result will be greatly superior to the dried, manufactured product. Failing that, though, fresh pasta is now more readily available from delicatessens, specialist Italian shops, and supermarkets.

Constructing a menu

The Italian way of eating is to start with an *antipasto*, such as stuffed vegetables, salami or seafood salad. A soup, or *minestra*, or a pasta usually follows, but not usually both. And then there is sometimes a vegetable course, though this is not essential. The *piatto di mezzo* follows, which means the middle dish, or main course, and is usually made up of meat or poultry or fish, often accompanied by a salad, or, rather more rarely, a vegetable.

Finally, there is the dessert. Desserts are very important in Italy. They may consist of nothing more complicated than fresh fruit in season, or they often entail a delicious ice-cream — no one makes better ones than the Italians — or there may be an elaborate pudding or cake.

Either way, the dessert is usually the meal's finishing touch, and cheese is rarely served at this stage. Cheese is more commonly served as part of the antipasto, or as a snack at some other point of the day.

Meals are always a great social event in Italy. The occasion brings everyone together, from the youngest member of the family to the oldest.

Lunch is probably the most important meal of the day, and people devote two hours to it. Factories and shops close down and everyone rushes home or, if they live too far away, they make their way to a favourite restaurant. Lunch consists of several courses, all equally important.

Pizza

Mention Italian food and most people think straight away of pizzas. Pizzas can be served as a meal, or can stave off hunger in the form of a quick and easy snack.

Naples is reputed to be the original home of the pizza, and is considered to be the culinary centre of the south. Pizzas are now found all over Italy and are baked in open brick ovens in pizzerias and bakeries.

Wine

Italy is the largest wine producer in the world. It is also high in the world's drinking league, with some 120 bottles being consumed per person per year.

There is an increasing number of Italian wines that are now available outside Italy. Every region makes its own wine. Piemonte is where Barolo comes from — a robust red wine to serve with roast meat and game — as well as the delicious Barbera, perfect fare for drinking with pasta and pizzas. Veneto produces Valpolicella and Soave, while Tuscany is home to Italy's most famous wine, Chianti Classico. Chianti is also an excellent wine to drink with roasts, grills and game dishes. Fortified wines, such as dry white vermouth and Marsala, are stronger than table wine

and are very good when used in the cooking process, during which they will impart an excellent flavour.

Fresh stock recipes

You will find it very useful to refer to these basic recipes as they are required throughout the book.

A good, flavoursome stock is easy, satisfying and cheap to make, and uses only a few basic ingredients. It is really not necessary to resort to stock cubes, when the flavour of a deliciously fresh, aromatic, broth is far superior. If you are making beef or fish stock you should be able to find the bones you need at your butcher or fishmonger.

Once made, the stocks can be frozen when cooled. Freeze in small batches in plastic tubs or ice cube trays. When frozen, the cubes can be transferred to clearly labelled plastic bags for ease of storage.

Every cook should be aware that a few basic rules are necessary in the making of a good stock. If you follow them, you will find that your finished dishes will taste much better. Also, you will never have to use a commercially made stock cube if you prefer not to.
• Stock should always simmer extremely gently, or it will evaporate too quickly and become cloudy.

• never add salt to the stock as simmering will reduce it and concentrate the flavour. This will affect the flavour of the finished dish.
• Any scum that rises to the surface should be removed as it appears, otherwise it will spoil the colour and flavour of the final stock.
• Avoid any floury root vegetables as these will cause the stock to become cloudy.

Beef stock
• Put 2.5 kg/5 lb beef or beef and veal bones in a roasting pan, and place in a preheated oven
230° C/450° F/Gas Mark 8. Roast for 1 hour or until browned and the fat and juices run out. Using a slotted spoon, transfer the bones to a large pot.
• Place the roasting pan on top of the stove, add 2 onions roughly chopped, 2 carrots roughly chopped and 2 celery stalks roughly chopped. Fry gently in the remaining fat until nicely browned, but do not burn. Add the vegetables to the bones in the saucepan together with 2 bay leaves, a few parsley stalks, 2 sprigs thyme, 10 whole peppercorns and cover with 4.8 litres/8 pints cold water.
• Bring to the boil, skim any scum from the surface, reduce the heat and simmer, uncovered, for 8 hours, skimming occasionally. Strain and cool, then refrigerate. Remove any fat on the surface.

Makes about 2.7 litres/ 4½ pints
Preparation time: 5–10 minutes
Cooking time: about 9 hours

"The one thing that all the regions of Italy have in common is their joyful approach to food and cooking."

Chicken stock
• Chop a cooked chicken carcass into 3 or 4 pieces and place it in a large pot with the raw giblets and trimmings, 1 onion roughly chopped, 2 large carrots roughly chopped, and 1 celery stalk roughly chopped, 1 bay leaf, a few parsley stalks, lightly crushed, 1 sprig thyme and cover with 1.8 litres/3 pints cold water.
• bring to the boil, removing any scum from the surface. Lower the heat and simmer for 2–2½ hours. Strain the stock through a muslin-lined sieve and leave to cool.

Makes 1 litre/ 1¾ pints
Preparation time: 5–10 minutes
Cooking time: about 2½ hours

Fish stock
Please note that when you are purchasing the bones for this stock, you should avoid the bones of oily fish. It is also very important that the stock does not boil

• Place 1½ kg/3 lb fish trimmings and 1 onion, sliced, white part of a small leek, 1 celery stalk, 1 bay leaf, 6 parsley stalks, 10 whole peppercorns and 475 ml/16 fl oz dry white wine into a large pot, and cover with 1.8 litres/3 pints cold water.

• Bring slowly to just below boiling point. Simmer for 20 minutes, removing any scum from the surface. Strain the stock through a muslin-lined sieve and leave to cool completely before refrigerating.

Makes 1.8 litres/ 3 pints
Preparation time: 10 minutes
Cooking time: 20 minutes

Vegetable stock
This recipe for vegetable stock can be varied to your own taste, and adapted according to what vegetables you have available. For example, you can try adding some fennel bulb for a mild aniseed flavour, or a sliver of orange zest for an added lift. The addition of tomatoes will give the finished stock extra richness of flavour and colour. Remember to avoid using any floury root vegetables as these will cause the stock to become cloudy.
• Place 500 g/1lb chopped mixed vegetables ie.carrots, leeks, celery,onion and mushrooms, about an equal quantity of each; 1 clove garlic, 6 peppercorns, 1 bouquet garni (2 parsley sprigs, 2 sprigs thyme and 1 bay leaf) in a pan, and cover with 1.2 litres/2 pints water.
• Bring to the boil and simmer gently for 30 minutes, skimming off any scum when necessary. Strain, and cool the stock completely before refrigerating.

Makes 1 litre/1¾ pints
Preparation time: 5–10 minutes
Cooking time: about 45 minutes

Cook's tools

> *"It is not really an exaggeration to say that peace and happiness begin, geographically, where garlic is used in cooking."*
>
> *Marcel Boulestin*

The gentle art of cooking is not for the faint-hearted. But if the cook can stand the heat in the kitchen, so must the tools he or she chooses and uses. Safe in the dishwasher, smooth, stainless steel saucepans, cool, marble chopping blocks, sharp, cooks' knives, blenders and whisks all form part of the "batterie de cuisine" of any chef worth his or her salt. Here are some basic guidelines, but the golden rule is to buy the best quality utensils you can afford!

Colander

Colanders are used for separating liquids and solids, and for draining and rinsing food. They come in many different shapes and sizes, but a colander is basically a container with holes in it. It is usually made of metal or plastic. Buy a colander which is big enough to hold the vegetables but not too large to rest in your sink.

Pizza/Pasta cutter

As the name suggests this is a useful implement for cutting pizzas, pastry or pasta. When choosing a cutter ensure that the wheel turns freely and that there is a guard to protect your fingers. The wheel should be stainless steel and the handle should be made from wood, metal or plastic.

Grater

Graters come in both a box shape or a single flat sheet. Both shapes have perforations which perform different functions. The fine holes are for grating spices and rind, the medium and large holes are for grating cheese and vegetables. Graters are generally made of stainless steel, as it is hard wearing and does not rust. Special parmesan graters are available too. These have a drawer underneath to catch the finely grated hard cheese. If you have a flat sheet grater, ensure that the grater is properly balanced when grating, as they do have a tendency to slip.

Measuring jug

A measuring jug is a standardised measure of liquid. It has a handle and a good pouring lip. Normally it is marked in both metric and imperial measures, fractions of pints, and fluid ounces as well as millilitres and litres. Jugs are available in glass, plastic or stainless steel. However, it is advisable to check before purchasing a jug that it is dishwasher safe.

Pasta server

A pasta server is a large stainless steel spoon with a long handle, used for transferring pasta or noodles from the pan to the serving dish. It has characteristic teeth which pick up spaghetti and tagliatelle easily and a hole which lets liquid drain away.

Pizza Brick or Stone

This is used to bake pizza or flat bread instead of a baking tray. It is not essential but it is very useful for authentic, even, cooking. It is made of terracotta brick as this retains the heat well and also crisps the bottom of the pizza during baking.

Garlic Press

A garlic press is used to finely crush garlic cloves by forcing the flesh through holes. This releases the oils and the full flavour of the garlic into the dish. This useful tool also saves the pungent aroma of garlic lingering on the skin, as you do not have to handle the juices from the crushed garlic.

Pizza slice

A pizza slice is a wide bladed slice which helps lift and transfer the pizza from the baking sheet to the serving dish. It is generally made of stainless steel. .

Palette Knife

A palette knife is a flexible, round bladed knife with no sharp edges. It is principally used as a smoothing or scraping implement, and is very handy in baking. The best palette knives are made of stainless steel, but they are also available made from rigid plastic.

Special utensils

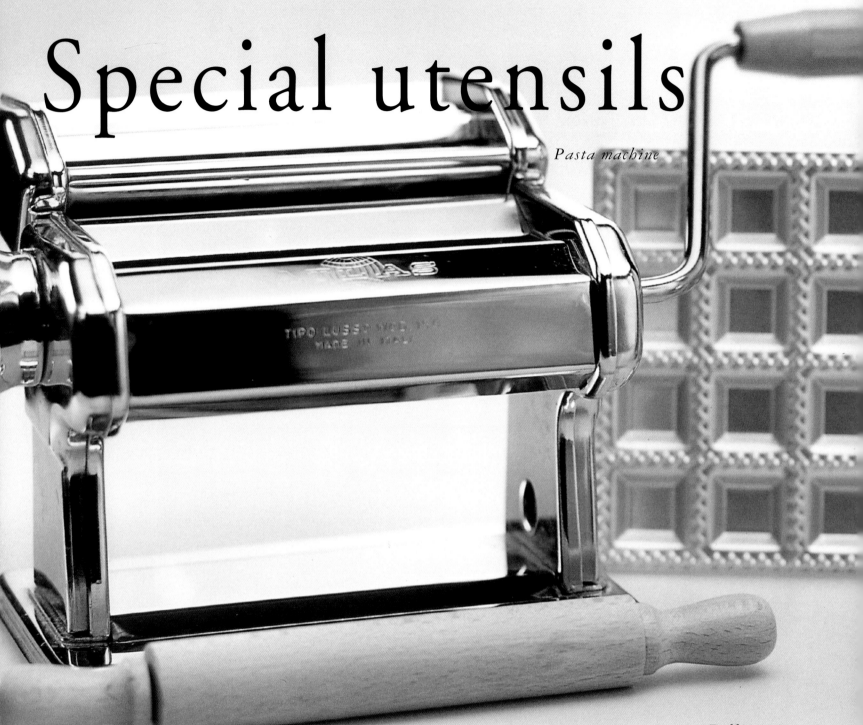

Pasta machine

Rolling pin

Pasta machine

If you make pasta regularly it is worth investing in a pasta machine which will ease the making of noodles and pasta considerably. The dough mixture is fed into the machine through the rollers until it comes out in a smooth elastic sheet. This process may have to be repeated several times. It is possible to buy attachments for a basic machine which will cut the flat sheet of dough into ribbons of tagliatelle and other pasta widths.

Rolling pin

A rolling pin is used for rolling out pasta and bread dough or pastry, to a smooth, flat, even sheet. It should be sufficiently heavy in order that it does the work rather than you. A rolling pin can be made of wood, plastic, nylon, or marble and should be wide and well balanced. When rolling out a dough or pastry mixture, use flour to stop the mixture sticking to the pin. Also, wipe the rolling pin clean prior to storing it.

Ravioli pan

Olive oil canister

Ravioli mould

Ravioli pan
A ravioli pan is a metal tray mould with indentations to make the ravioli shapes. A small rolling pin is usually provided in order to push out the ravioli.

Ravioli mould
A ravioli mould is a single mould used to press out two shapes of ravioli from the pasta sheet. The pasta is then filled with the chosen stuffing.

Olive oil canister
This canister has a particularly long, thin spout which is useful for distributing oil evenly over salads, pans and utensils. It ensures that there is no unnecessary wastage. It is best to invest in a small canister to use while you are cooking, but you should not store oil in this way, as it spoils the oil and corrodes the canister.

Soups and Antipasti

Courgette Soup
with Parmesan crostini

This is a fresh, light-textured soup with a delicate flavour. It can be made any time of year, since courgettes are readily available.

40 g/1½ oz butter
1 onion, sliced
500 g/1 lb courgettes, thinly sliced
1.2 litres/2 pints Chicken Stock (see page 11)
2 small eggs
2 tablespoons grated Parmesan cheese
1 tablespoon chopped basil or parsley
salt and pepper
crostini or croûtons, to garnish

melt the butter in a saucepan, add the onion and fry gently for 5 minutes. Add the courgettes and fry, stirring frequently for 5–10 minutes. Add the chicken stock, bring to the boil, cover and simmer for 20 minutes.

purée in an electric blender or rub through a sieve. Return to the saucepan and bring to the boil.

beat together the eggs, cheese and herbs in a warmed soup tureen, then slowly beat in the boiling soup. Check the seasoning and pour into individual soup bowls.

garnish with crostini or croûtons and serve immediately.

Serves 4–6
Preparation time: *25–30 minutes*
Cooking time: *20 minutes*

clipboard: To make crostini, cut round bread rolls into 5 mm/¼ inch thick slices and toast one side. Spread the untoasted side with butter, sprinkle thickly with grated cheese and place under a preheated hot grill until golden and bubbling.

Country-style Minestrone

This is one of the best known Italian soups, a hearty, warming, peasant dish, substantial enough to provide a whole meal in itself.

125 g/4 oz cannellini beans
3 tablespoons oil
2 onions, chopped
2 garlic cloves, crushed
2–3 rindless bacon rashers, chopped
1.8 litres/3 pints water
1 teaspoon chopped fresh marjoram
½ teaspoon chopped fresh thyme
4 tomatoes, skinned (see clipboard below), deseeded and chopped
2 carrots, diced
2 potatoes, diced
1 small turnip, diced
1–2 celery sticks
250 g/8 oz cabbage
50 g/2 oz small pasta shapes
3 tablespoons grated Parmesan cheese, plus extra to serve
salt and freshly ground pepper

To garnish
1 teaspoon chopped fresh parsley
sprig fresh thyme, to garnish

place the cannellini beans in a large bowl and cover with water. Leave them to soak for 8 hours or overnight. Drain the beans and then rinse under running cold water.

heat the oil in a large saucepan and add the onions, garlic and bacon. Sauté gently for about 5 minutes, stirring occasionally, until the onions are soft and golden brown.

add the beans, water, herbs and tomatoes, cover the pan and simmer gently for 2 hours. Add the carrots and simmer for 10 minutes. Stir in the potatoes and turnip and cook for another 10 minutes.

chop the celery and shred the cabbage. Add to the soup with the pasta shapes and cook for 10 minutes, or until the pasta and all the vegetables are tender. Season to taste. Stir in the Parmesan and then ladle into individual soup bowls. Serve immediately, sprinkled with extra Parmesan and garnish with fresh parsley and thyme.

Serves 6
Preparation time: *20 minutes, plus soaking overnight*
Cooking time: *2½ hours*

clipboard: to skin tomatoes, place them in a bowl and pour over enough boiling water to cover. Leave for 1–2 minutes, then drain, cut a cross at the stem end of each tomato, and peel off the skins.

Smoked Ham and Bean Soup

scented with garlic

375 g/12 oz dried borlotti or cannellini beans
1 carrot, chopped
1 onion, quartered
1 bouquet garni
125 g/4 oz cooked smoked ham, cubed
2 shallots, finely chopped
1 garlic clove, crushed
40 g/1½ oz butter
1 tablespoon chopped parsley
salt and freshly ground black pepper
½ tablespoon chopped parsley, to garnish
125 g/4 oz croûtons, to serve

soak the beans overnight in cold water, drain. Bring the beans to the boil over a medium heat in a large pan with 2 litres/3½ pints lightly salted water. Add the carrot, onion, bouquet garni and ham. Leave to simmer for 2 hours, or until the beans are tender.

put the soup in a blender or food processor, first removing the bouquet garni. Return the purée to the pan and reheat over a medium heat.

cook the shallots and garlic in the butter in a heavy pan, when golden add the chopped parsley and mix quickly. Turn off the heat and add this mixture to the bean purée.

mix well with a wooden spoon, add a good sprinkling of pepper and the extra parsley, then pour into individual bowls. Serve the croûtons separately.

Serves 4
Preparation time: *30 minutes, plus overnight soaking*
Cooking time: *2 hours*

Salamis and sausages

Parma Ham

Pancetta

Fresh Italian Sausage

Mortadello

Parma Ham
Parma ham (or Prosciutto) comes from Parma. Because of its long curing process the ham commands a high price. Parma ham is pink in colour and marbled with white fat,. It is sliced wafer thin and is often served with melon or figs as an antipasto.

Pancetta
Pancetta is unsmoked bacon taken from the belly of a pig. It is cured with spices, salt and pepper. The bacon is then rolled into a sausage shape and sliced very thinly. Pancetta is also very popular diced and fried with garlic and onions.

Fresh Italian Sausage
Italian fresh sausages are made in various shapes and sizes and spiced with garlic, pepper, fennel and wine. Salamelle and Zampone are typical examples. They are traditionally poached whole and are served hot with potato salad or vegetables.

Mortadello
Mortadello is a large, slightly smoked sausage made from pure pork or a mixture of meats. It is seasoned with parsley and studded with olives and pistachio nuts. It is thinly sliced or diced and eaten cold in sandwiches or salads.

Spinata Romana

Bresaola

Bocconcino

Ferrara Salami

Bocconcino
Bocconcino are small, sausage-shaped salamis sold in a string. They are made of raw pork or other red meat interspersed with fat and are highly seasoned. Bocconcino should be sliced very finely and used in salads and sandwiches.

Bresaola
Bresaola is a high quality salted, raw beef which is very expensive as it goes through a long, complicated curing process. It is served in very thin slices as an antipasto and is delicious with a simple dressing of olive oil, lemon juice and pepper.

Ferrara Salami
Ferrara salami is one of the countless varieties of regional Italian salamis. It is a large salami made of raw meat which has been seasoned with garlic and pepper. It is served sliced as an antipasto and is also good in sandwiches and as an addition to salads.

Spinata Romana
Spinata Romana is a speciality of the countryside around Rome. It is a large square-shaped salami with a distinctive appearance, papery texture and a mild taste. It is studded through with large chunks of pork fat and peppercorns.

White Bean
and vermicelli soup

A nourishing, country-style soup to serve on cold winter evenings.

250 g/8 oz dried borlotti or cannellini beans, soaked overnight
250 g/8 oz pork belly with skin
1 onion, finely chopped
1 carrot, finely chopped
1 celery stick, finely chopped
1 garlic clove, crushed
3 parsley sprigs, finely chopped
1 sprig of sage, chopped
1 bay leaf
175 g/6 oz vermicelli, spaghetti or ribbon noodles
2 tablespoons olive oil
salt and freshly ground black pepper

drain the beans and put in a large saucepan with the pork, onion, carrot, celery, garlic, parsley, sage, bay leaf and enough water to cover. Bring to the boil, then reduce the heat, cover the pan and simmer gently for 2 hours, or until the beans are soft.

put one cupful of beans through a food mill or rub through a sieve. Stir the puréed beans back into the soup. Season to taste with salt and pepper and bring back to the boil.

add the vermicelli, spaghetti or noodles and boil for about 12 minutes, or until the pasta is cooked and tender, but still firm to the bite (*al dente*).

remove the pork from the soup. Cut off the rind and cut the meat into small pieces. Just before serving, drizzle the olive oil into the soup and stir in the pork and a generous grinding of black pepper. Transfer to a tureen or individual serving dishes.

Serves 4–6
Preparation time: *20 minutes plus soaking overnight*
Cooking time: *2½ hours*

clipboard: This is one of many versions of soups made with different kinds of dried beans combined with pasta or noodles. These soups are usually described as *pasta con fagioli* or *pasta e fagioli*.

Garlic Crostini
with chicken liver pâté

These crunchy titbits are special enough to prepare as a light snack in themselves, as well as being a delicious first course for a dinner party.

50 g/2 oz butter
I small onion, finely chopped
I–2 garlic cloves, crushed
250 g/8 oz chicken livers, trimmed of all sinew
2 anchovy fillets
I tablespoon cream
2–3 tablespoons Marsala
pinch of paprika
12 x I cm/½ inch slices of bread cut diagonally from a small French loaf
olive oil for frying
2–3 extra garlic cloves, halved
salt and pepper
I tablespoon chopped parsley, to serve
small amount of paprika to garnish (optional)

heat the butter in a frying pan and cook the onion and garlic until soft but not coloured. Add the chicken livers and cook gently for about 10 minutes until they are just coloured, then add the anchovy fillets.

purée the liver mixture in a food processor or liquidizer until smooth. Add the cream and sufficient Marsala to give a soft, spreadable consistency. Add the paprika and season to taste. Keep hot.

fry the slices of bread in hot olive oil until golden brown on both sides. Rub the garlic over one surface of each slice of bread and cover with the liver pâté.

sprinkle a little chopped parsley and a little paprika, if liked, over each slice just before serving. Serve hot.

Serves 4
Preparation time: *20 minutes*
Cooking time: *20–30 minutes*

clipboard: Instead of frying the bread, rub the garlic over each slice of bread, then dip the bread into olive oil and place on a baking tray. Bake in a preheated hot oven at 230°C/450°F/Gas Mark 8 for 12–15 minutes or until golden brown. Turn once or twice during baking so that the bread colours on both sides.

Vegetable Antipasto
with peppers and leeks

This is a wonderfully tasty appetizer, combining the smoky taste of grilled peppers and pungent leeks. Fresh vegetables are very much in keeping with new trends in healthy eating.

For the pepper salad
4 red, green and yellow peppers

4 tablespoons olive oil

1 tablespoon chopped, fresh parsley

2 garlic cloves, crushed or chopped

freshly ground sea salt

For the leeks in vinaigrette
500 g/1 lb thin leeks, washed and trimmed

6 tablespoons olive oil

1 tablespoon lemon juice

2 tablespoons balsamic or wine vinegar

2 garlic cloves, crushed

sea salt and freshly ground black pepper

place the peppers under a hot grill and cook them until they are black and blistered. Turn them occasionally to cook them evenly on all sides. Place in a polythene bag until they are cool, and then peel away the skins.

cut the peppers open and remove all the seeds. Cut the flesh into thin strips and arrange them on a serving dish, Sprinkle with olive oil and scatter with parsley and garlic. Finally, sprinkle a little sea salt over the peppers.

cook the leeks in a large saucepan of lightly salted boiling water for about 10 minutes or until they are tender but still firm. Drain them thoroughly in a colander, and transfer them to a serving dish.

make the vinaigrette: mix together the olive oil, lemon juice, vinegar, garlic and seasoning until well blended. Pour the dressing over the leeks and serve either warm or cold with the pepper salad and some fresh ciabatta or crusty bread.

Serves 4–6
Preparation time: *30 minutes*
Cooking time: *15 minutes*

Parma Ham

with figs or melon

Parma Ham or Prosciutto is prized in Italy in the same way as Scottish salmon is in Britain. It combines beautifully with fresh figs or melon, and is a perfect starter.

8 ripe purple figs
4 slices Parma ham or raw smoked ham
freshly ground black pepper, to season

Variation
1 sweet ripe melon, chilled
4 slices Parma ham, or raw smoked ham
freshly ground black pepper, to serve

cut the figs almost through into quarters.

arrange the ham on individual plates and top with the figs. Serve with freshly ground black pepper.

Variation
cut the melon into quarters and remove the seeds.

drape the slices of ham over the melon. Serve with freshly ground black pepper.

Serves 4
Preparation time: *10 minutes*

clipboard: This is the easiest of all *antipasti* to prepare, yet, because of its simplicity, the ingredients must be of the finest quality. Experiment with different kinds of melons, Galia is used here, but Charentais is also deliciously fragrant. There is also a variety of smoked hams available, some less expensive than Parma. Coppa, and coppa crudo (ham from the shoulder) are delicious, and won't cost as much.

Onion Savoury

on Italian bread

Some of the traditional Italian breads such as ciabatta and focaccia are made with olive oil, and these make the perfect base for this aromatic savoury. You can also serve it as a tasty snack with soup.

750 g/1½ lb onions, sliced
2 tablespoons olive oil
125 g/4 oz bacon, chopped
few basil leaves, torn
375 g/12 oz tomatoes, skinned (see page 20) and mashed
3 eggs, beaten
75 g/3 oz Parmesan cheese, grated
4 slices of hot toasted olive oil bread eg: ciabatta or focaccia
salt and pepper
extra basil leaves, shredded, to garnish

put the onions in a bowl, cover with cold water and soak overnight.

heat the oil in a large, heavy-based pan, add the bacon and fry gently until browned. Drain the onions thoroughly, then add to the pan with the basil and salt and pepper to taste. Cook over low heat for 20 minutes, stirring occasionally.

add the tomatoes, cover the pan, lower the heat and cook very gently for 10 minutes. Taste and adjust the seasoning. Beat the eggs and Parmesan together, then add to the pan. Remove from the heat immediately and stir vigorously.

put a slice of hot toast in each individual soup bowl, then spoon over the hot savoury. Serve immediately, garnished with basil.

Serves 4
Preparation time: *20 minutes, plus overnight soaking*
Cooking time: *30 minutes*

clipboard: You can make your own olive oil bread easily if you prefer (see pages 248-250). Otherwise, it is available in large supermarkets. This savoury is a good way of using up bread that is a couple of days old.

Fish and Shellfish

Fresh Sardines
with pine nuts and anchovies

75–100 ml/3–3½ fl oz olive oil
250 g/8 oz fresh white breadcrumbs
40 g/1½ oz sultanas, soaked in hot water and drained
40 g/1½ oz pine nuts
1 tablespoon chopped parsley
1 x 40 g/1½ oz can anchovies, drained and chopped
pinch of nutmeg
750 g/1½ lb sardines, heads and backbones removed
approximately 12 bay leaves
4 tablespoons lemon juice
salt and pepper

To garnish
lemon wedges

heat 4–5 tablespoons of oil in a frying pan and fry half the breadcrumbs over moderate heat, turning them frequently with a metal spatula until they are a light golden brown.

remove from the heat and add the sultanas, pine nuts, parsley, anchovies and nutmeg. Season to taste with salt and pepper.

place a little of the mixture inside each sardine and press the sides together to close. Arrange rows of sardines in a single layer in a large oiled oven-to-table dish. Place half a bay leaf between each sardine.

sprinkle the remaining breadcrumbs and the oil over the top and bake in a preheated oven at 180°C/350°F/Gas Mark 4 for 30 minutes. Sprinkle the lemon juice over the top just before serving. Serve hot, garnished with lemon wedges.

Serves 4
Preparation time: *30–35 minutes*
Cooking time: *40–50 minutes*
Oven temperature:180°C/350°F/Gas Mark 4

clipboard: If fresh sardines are not available, sprats or small pilchards can be used instead.

Baby Squid
with spinach and tomatoes

2–3 tablespoons olive oil

1 onion, chopped

1–2 garlic cloves, crushed

1 fresh chilli, chopped

1 stick celery, chopped

2 tablespoons chopped parsley, plus extra to garnish

600 g/1¼ lb baby squid, cleaned and cut into 1 cm/½ inch slices

2 teaspoons plain flour

100 g/4 oz mushrooms, quartered or thickly sliced

375 g/12 oz large tomatoes, peeled, deseeded and chopped

500 g/1 lb fresh spinach, chopped

300 ml/½ pint dry white wine

salt and pepper

heat the oil in a large pan and add the onions, garlic, chilli and celery, and cook gently until the onion is golden brown,

add the parsley and squid, and cook gently for a further 10 minutes. Stir in the flour, mix well and then add the mushrooms, tomatoes, spinach and white wine. Season to taste with salt and pepper.

cover and simmer very gently for about 30 minutes or until the squid is nearly cooked, then remove the lid and simmer until the sauce thickens and the squid is completely tender.

check the seasoning and pour into a hot serving dish. Serve hot, garnished with the extra chopped parsley.

Serves 4
Preparation time: *30–35 minutes*
Cooking time: *50–55 minutes*

clipboard: Squid may be bought already cleaned; if not, your fishmonger may do it for you. Squid must be cooked very gently if it is not to become rubbery. Length of cooking time will depend on size. For the best results with this dish, choose baby squid.

Saffron Fish
with sweet peppers and tomatoes

This is a delicious way of cooking firm, white-fleshed fish such as cod. It makes a fragrant, aromatic dish.

½ teaspoon saffron strands
625 g/1¼ lb cod fillet or other firm white fish
1 tablespoon flour
3 tablespoons oil
2 sweet yellow peppers, deseeded and cut into strips
2 tomatoes, chopped
1 small onion, finely chopped
1 garlic clove, finely chopped
1 tablespoon chopped parsley
salt and pepper
slices of polenta, to serve (optional)

put the saffron strands to soak in a little hot water.

cut the fish fillets into even-sized pieces and dust with flour. Heat the oil in a large shallow pan, add the cod and cook over medium heat for a few minutes, turning once until golden.

season with salt and pepper, remove with a fish slice and keep warm.

add the prepared vegetables to the pan and cook, stirring until golden. Season with a pinch of salt, reduce the heat, cover with a lid and simmer for about 30 minutes.

stir in the saffron liquid halfway though.

when the vegetables are almost cooked, add the pieces of cod and sprinkle with chopped parsley. Serve hot with slices of polenta, if liked.

Serves 4
Preparation time: *10 minutes*
Cooking time: *35 minutes*

clipboard: Polenta is warming and filling, and is Italian equivalent of mashed potatoes. Made from maize flour, it can be eaten cold, in slices.

Fresh Tuna
with anchovies and mushrooms

Tuna is very popular in Italy, and appears in many traditional dishes. This recipe is simple, elegant and gratifyingly easy to prepare.

4–6 tablespoons oil
2–3 garlic cloves, crushed
1 large onion, finely chopped
150 g/5 oz button mushrooms, quartered or thickly sliced
6–8 anchovy fillets, chopped
2 tablespoons chopped parsley
1 tablespoon plain flour
300 ml/10 fl oz dry white wine
pepper
pinch of nutmeg
4 x 150–225 g/6–8 oz tuna steaks, about 1 cm/½ inch thick

heat the oil in a pan and cook the garlic and onion until soft and lightly coloured. Add the mushrooms and cook for 2–3 minutes, then add the anchovies, parsley and flour. Mix together well.

stir in the wine, bring to the boil, stirring all the time, then simmer gently for 5–7 minutes.

season to taste with pepper and a pinch of nutmeg. There should be no need to add salt because the anchovies are salty.

place the tuna steaks in an oven-to-table dish and pour over the sauce.

cover with a lid or foil and cook in a preheated oven at 190°C/375°F/Gas Mark 5 for 40–45 minutes. Serve hot.

Serves 4
Preparation time: *15–20 minutes*
Cooking time: *55–60 minutes*
Oven temperature: *190°C/375°F/Gas Mark 5*

clipboard: Swordfish or halibut steaks could equally well be used in this recipe, in place of tuna.

Fish Steaks
with tomato and garlic sauce

4 x 150 g/5 oz white fish steaks, such as sea bass,
John Dory or monkfish
3 tablespoons olive oil

Marinade
5 tablespoons olive oil
juice of ½ lemon
1 tablespoon finely chopped fresh parsley

Tomato sauce
2 tablespoons olive oil
4 garlic cloves, chopped
750g/1½ lb tomatoes, skinned (see page 20)
and chopped
4 anchovy fillets, chopped
salt and freshly ground black pepper
1 tablespoon chopped oregano, to garnish

wash the fish steaks under running cold water and pat them dry with absorbent kitchen paper. Put all the marinade ingredients in a bowl and mix together well.

add the white fish steaks to the marinade, turning them until they are thoroughly coated and glistening with oil. Cover the bowl and leave in a cool place for at least 1 hour.

heat the olive oil in a large frying pan. Remove the fish steaks from the marinade and fry gently until they are cooked and golden brown on both sides, turning the fish once during cooking. Remove the steaks from the pan and keep them warm.

while the fish steaks are cooking, make the tomato sauce. Heat the olive oil in a pan and sauté the garlic until just golden.

add the tomatoes and chopped anchovies, and cook over medium heat until the tomatoes are reduced to a thick pulpy consistency.

season to taste with salt and pepper. Pour the sauce over the fish and sprinkle with oregano.

Serves 4
Preparation time: *15 minutes, plus 1 hour marinating*
Cooking time: *15 minutes*

Marsala Sole
with Parmesan cheese

The cheese and wine in this recipe make a rich, luxurious sauce for the fish. Ideally, Dover sole should be used, as it is the finest quality. Lemon sole makes a perfectly good substitute, but it will have a different flavour.

flour for dusting
4 medium Dover or lemon sole, skinned
75 g/3 oz butter
25 g/1 oz grated Parmesan cheese
50 ml/2 fl oz Fish Stock (see page 11)
3 tablespoons Marsala or white wine
salt and freshly ground black pepper

To serve
grated Parmesan cheese
sprigs of flat-leaved parsley
lemon wedges

put some flour in a shallow bowl and season with salt and pepper. Dip the sole into the seasoned flour to dust them lightly on both sides. Shake off any excess flour.

heat the butter in a large frying pan. Add the floured Dover sole and cook over gentle heat until they are golden brown on both sides, turning them once during cooking.

sprinkle the grated Parmesan over the sole and then cook very gently for another 2–3 minutes until the cheese melts.

add the fish stock and the Marsala or white wine. Cover the pan and cook over very low heat for 4–5 minutes, until the sole are cooked and tender and the sauce reduced. Serve sprinkled with grated Parmesan and garnish with lemon wedges.

Serves 4
Preparation time: *5 minutes*
Cooking time: *12 minutes*

Sicilian Fish Stew
with black olives

Sicily abounds in sardines, tuna, swordfish, grey mullet and cod. Mussels are also plentiful, and feature in many dishes.

300 ml/½ pint mussels
75 ml/3 fl oz olive oil
1 onion, finely sliced
2 garlic cloves, crushed
2 carrots, cut into strips
425 g/14 oz canned chopped tomatoes
125 g/4 oz black olives
1 bay leaf
4 slices of white bread
1 kg/2 lb mixed fish (e.g. white fish, red mullet, scallops, prawns) prepared or cut into chunks
salt and freshly ground black pepper
2 tablespoons fresh parsley, finely chopped, to garnish

prepare the mussels: cover with cold water and discard any that are open, or rise to the surface. Scrub well to remove any barnacles, remove the beards and soak in fresh cold water until ready to cook.

heat 2 tablespoons of the olive oil in a heavy-based frying pan, and sauté the onion, garlic and carrots for about 5 minutes or until soft. Add the tomatoes with their juice, black olives and bay leaf, and season with salt and black pepper. Simmer gently for 15 minutes.

cut four large circles from the slices of bread. Heat the remaining oil in a small frying pan and then sauté the bread until crisp and golden on both sides. Remove, drain on absorbent kitchen paper and keep warm.

add the prepared fish to the stew and cook for 5 minutes. Add the mussels and simmer for 10 minutes or until the shells open. Discard any that do not open. Remove the bay leaf. Put a piece of fried bread in the bottom of each of 4 warm deep plates or large shallow soup bowls. Ladle the fish stew over the top. Sprinkle with chopped parsley and serve immediately with plenty of crusty bread.

Serves 4
Preparation time: *30 minutes*
Cooking time: *35 minutes*

King Prawns
in a cream and mustard sauce

*This is a luxuriously rich recipe and uses the finest king prawns, so it is a good choice for special occasions.
If you can get it, use Grappa which is a good, strong Italian brandy.*

50 g/2 oz butter
24 king-sized uncooked prawns, shelled
2 tablespoons Grappa or other brandy
225 ml/7½ fl oz double cream
2–3 teaspoons French mustard
salt and white pepper

To garnish
1 tablespoon chopped parsley
lemon wedges

heat the butter in a frying pan and cook the prawns for a few minutes. Warm the brandy, pour over the prawns and set alight.

when the flames have subsided, stir in the cream. Season to taste with the mustard, salt and pepper.

simmer very gently for 4–5 minutes until the prawns are tender, making sure that they do not become tough.

pour into a hot serving dish and sprinkle with chopped parsley before serving with boiled rice.

Serves 4
Preparation time: *15 minutes*
Cooking time: *12–15 minutes*

clipboard: For a less expensive dish, use 500 g/1 lb peeled prawns. In this case, boil the cream first for 4–5 minutes until it thickens slightly. Heat the prawns in the butter, flambé with brandy, pour the cream over, season to taste with mustard, salt and pepper, and serve immediately.

Frittura Mista
from the catch of the day

The Adriatic waters yield a variety of fish, so when Italian fishermen get just a few of each kind in their nets, they cook them all together in this typical sea food fry-up.

125–175 g/4–6 oz prepared squid, sliced
125–175 g/4–6 oz whitebait
125–175 g/4–6 oz large prawns
125–175 g/4–6 oz plaice fillets, skinned and cut into
1 cm/½ inch strips
125 g/4 oz plain flour
salt and pepper
oil for deep frying

To garnish
1–2 lemons, sliced or quartered
few sprigs of flat-leaved parsley

wash all the fish and dry well with absorbent kitchen paper. Season the flour with salt and pepper.

heat the oil in a deep pan to 180°–190°C/350–375°F or until a cube of bread browns in 30 seconds.

toss the fish, a batch at a time, into the seasoned flour and fry until golden brown.

drain well on absorbent kitchen paper, place on a hot serving dish and keep hot.

sprinkle the fish lightly with salt and garnish the dish with lemon and parsley just before serving, .

Serves 4
Preparation time: *30–40 minutes*
Cooking time: *15–20 minutes*

clipboard: Any selection of small fish or pieces of fish can be used in this dish, such as queen scallops, pieces of skate or monkfish, cooked shelled mussels, or small peeled prawns.

Baked Mussels
with Parmesan and garlic

If your fishmonger has some good, fresh mussels available, try this recipe. It is a typically Italian way of preparing them.

2.4 litres/4 pints mussels
bouquet garni
125 ml/4 fl oz water
125 ml/4 fl oz dry white wine
2 tablespoons finely chopped shallot
1 garlic clove, crushed
2 tablespoons chopped fresh parsley
75 g/3 oz fresh breadcrumbs
3 tablespoons grated Parmesan cheese
25 g/1 oz butter
salt and freshly ground black pepper

prepare the mussels: place them in a bowl and cover them with cold water. Discard any that are open or rise to the surface. Scrub the mussels to remove any barnacles and remove the beards. Soak in fresh cold water until ready to cook. Drain well.

put the mussels in a deep saucepan with the bouquet garni, salt and pepper. Add the water and wine, cover the pan and cook over moderate heat until the mussels open, shaking the pan occasionally. Discard any mussels that do not open, then strain them and reserve the liquid.

remove the empty half of each mussel shell and arrange the remaining shells close together, mussel side up, in a shallow ovenproof baking dish. Sprinkle the mussels with the chopped shallot, garlic, parsley, breadcrumbs and Parmesan.

reduce the mussel liquid to half its original volume by boiling rapidly. Pour the reduced liquid around the mussels and dot with butter. Bake in a preheated oven at 180°C/350°F/Gas Mark 4 for 15 minutes. Serve at once.

Serves 4
Preparation time: *30 minutes*
Cooking time: *15–20 minutes*
Oven temperature: *180°C/350°F/Gas Mark 4*

Grilled Mussels
with tomatoes and peppers

These grilled mussels make a colourful and inexpensive starter, and they are really easy and quick to cook.

2.4 litres/4 pints mussels
200 ml/7 fl oz white wine
½ red pepper, deseeded and chopped
2 garlic cloves, crushed
4 tablespoons fresh parsley,
finely chopped
425 g/14 oz can chopped tomatoes
5 tablespoons fresh white breadcrumbs
2 tablespoons olive oil
1 tablespoon grated Parmesan cheese
salt and freshly ground black pepper
fresh parsley, finely chopped, to garnish

prepare the mussels: cover with cold water and discard any that are open, or rise to the surface. Scrub them under running cold water to remove any barnacles and the beards. Put the cleaned mussels in a large saucepan with the wine and bring to the boil, covered with a close-fitting lid.

cook the mussels over medium heat for a few minutes, still covered and shaking the pan occasionally until the mussels open. Discard any mussels that do not open. Remove the open mussels from the pan and take off and throw away the top half of each shell.

mix together the chopped pepper, garlic, parsley, chopped tomatoes and 4 tablespoons of the breadcrumbs in a bowl. Stir in 1 tablespoon of the olive oil and then season to taste with salt and some freshly ground black pepper.

add a little of this mixture to each of the mussels in their shells and place them in an ovenproof dish. Sprinkle with grated Parmesan and the remaining breadcrumbs and olive oil and bake in a preheated oven at 230°C/150°F/Gas Mark 8 for 10 minutes. Preheat the grill and flash the mussels under the hot grill for a crisp finish. Sprinkle with parsley.

Serves 4–6
Preparation time: *30 minutes*
Cooking time: *10 minutes*
Oven temperature: *230°C/150°F/Gas Mark 8*

Pasta and Gnocchi

Fresh pasta

Cannelloni verde

Tagliarini

Lasagne

Ravioli

Christmas shapes

Cannelloni verde
Cannelloni consists of large, thin tubes of pasta which can be stuffed with a variety of different ingredients and served with a cheese sauce. It is often made with spinach, which colours it green .

Lasagne
Lasagne is very popular, and is made in flat broad sheets which are available fresh or dried. The sheets are usually cooked and layered with meat, cheese, vegetables and sauce and baked in the oven.

Christmas shapes
These are particularly appealing to children and are great for parties.

Tagliarini
Tagliarini consists of long, flat, ribbon-shaped noodles

rolled paper thin. They are often used in soups.

Ravioli
Ravioli is very popular. Two shapes of pasta are parcelled together and stuffed with meat, cheese or vegetables

Caramelle

Tortelloni

Agnolini

Linguine Verde

Cappelletti

and covered in a sauce. It is usually made in a half-moon shape when made at home in Italy. Fresh ravioli is best.

Caramelle
This fresh pasta is made in the shape of a sweet, often encasing a delicious stuffing

such as a mixture of spinach and ricotta cheese.

Tortelloni
Tortelloni is pinched into shapes which look like small ears. It is mostly stuffed with spinach and ricotta, and is served like ravioli with a

sauce or with butter and freshly ground pepper.

Agnolini
Agnolini is another pasta used with various stuffings. The small crescent shapes are cooked, then served with a meat or cream sauce.

Linguine Verde
Linguine is available fresh or dried, it is a flat ribbon noodle similar to fettucine.

Cappelletti
The 'little hats' can be filled with any suitable stuffing such as spinach, ricotta etc.

Fresh Pasta
to make at home

This makes a standard quantity of home-made fresh pasta.

300 g/10 oz strong plain flour, sifted
pinch of salt
3 eggs
1 tablespoon of olive oil
flour for dusting

put the flour and salt on a work surface. Make a well in the centre and add the eggs. Using the fingertips, draw the flour in from the sides and mix well. Add the olive oil and continue mixing until you have a soft dough. Alternatively, you can make the dough in a food processor.

turn out the dough on to a lightly floured surface and knead well until it is really smooth and silky. Roll out the dough, giving it an occasional quarter turn and stretching it out until it resembles a thick sheet of cloth and is almost transparent.

hang the pasta over the back of a chair or a broom handle and leave to dry for about 10 minutes. Alternatively, lay it out on a table with one-third overhanging the edge and keep turning it so that it dries out completely.

roll up the pasta loosely like a Swiss roll and then cut through horizontally at regular intervals to make fettuccine (3 mm/⅛ inch wide) or tagliatelle (5 mm/¼ inch wide). Unravel them and toss gently in a little flour. Leave them to dry on a cloth for at least 30 minutes before cooking in salted boiling water. Serve with a sauce or simply tossed with olive oil, garlic, salt and pepper and parsley.

Serves 4
Preparation time: *1 hour*
Cooking time: *2–3 minutes*

clipboard: To make lasagne or ravioli, cut the prepared pasta dough into sheets, as required, rather than strips.

Deep-fried Pasta *from Tuscany*

This is a traditional pasta recipe from the heart of Italy. These crisp, tasty puffs make excellent nibbles with drinks, and are ideal to serve with savoury sauces and dips.

½ teaspoon dried yeast
¼ teaspoon sugar
500 g/1 lb plain flour
25 g/1 oz butter
150 ml/¼ pint lukewarm Chicken Stock (see page 11)
vegetable oil for deep frying
salt and freshly ground black pepper

dissolve the yeast and sugar in a little water. Set aside for 10 minutes.

sift the flour and a little salt on to a work surface. Stir in the yeast mixture, then add the butter and enough stock to make a soft dough. Knead well, then roll out to a fairly thick sheet.

fold the 4 corners of the dough in towards the centre, then flatten with the rolling pin.

fold and flatten again at least 5 more times. Roll out to a sheet about 5 mm/¼ inch thick and cut into small rectangles.

deep fry the shapes a few at a time in hot oil until golden brown and puffed up. Drain on absorbent kitchen paper while frying the remainder. Sprinkle with salt and pepper, and serve hot.

Serves 6
Preparation time: *1 hour, plus 10 minutes resting*
Cooking time: *20–30 minutes, depending on the number of batches*

Penne
with chilli sauce

Pasta with chilli sauce is a true Italian classic. This recipe is not too hot, and once you've got used to the intense flavour of the chillies, you'll really enjoy it.

1–2 tablespoons olive oil
1 large onion, finely chopped
2 garlic cloves, crushed
125 g/4 oz rindless streaky bacon, chopped
1–2 fresh red chillies, chopped
1 x 400 g/14 oz can chopped tomatoes
50–75 g/2–3 oz pecorino or Parmesan cheese, shaved
500 g/1 lb penne
salt and pepper

heat the oil in a pan and cook the onion, garlic and bacon until they are lightly coloured.

add the chillies, tomatoes and 25 g/1 oz of the cheese. Season to taste with salt and pepper. Cook over a gentle heat for 30–40 minutes until the sauce thickens. Check the seasoning.

cook the penne in boiling salted water for about 12 minutes until just tender (*al dente*). Drain well and place in a hot serving dish.

stir in most of the sauce, mix well and then pour the remaining sauce over the top. Garnish with curls of pecorino or Parmesan, and serve the remaining cheese separately.

Serves 4
Preparation time: *15–20 minutes*
Cooking time: *50 minutes–1 hour*

clipboard: You can buy either red or green chillies, the red ones being hotter. For a milder taste, slice the chillies in half lengthways and scrape out the seeds with the point of a small knife before chopping them. Be careful not to touch your eyes or mouth and wash your hands well after handling chillies as the juice is very pungent.

Trenette

with anchovies and tomatoes

The anchovies in this recipe make a perfect blend with the peppers and tomatoes. It is an ideal dish to make from the store-cupboard.

4–6 tablespoons olive oil
2 garlic cloves, crushed
2 large onions, finely chopped
1 red pepper, skinned, deseeded and cut into strips
1 x 425 g/14 oz can chopped plum tomatoes
1 x 40 g/1½ oz can anchovies, drained and chopped
pinch of sugar
500 g/1 lb trenette
8 tablespoons grated Parmesan cheese
salt and pepper
1 tablespoon parsley, finely chopped, to garnish

heat half the oil in a pan and cook the garlic and onions until soft and just beginning to colour.

add the pepper strips and cook until soft, then add the tomatoes and anchovies, season with pepper and stir in the sugar. Cook for a few minutes longer until the tomatoes and anchovies are heated through.

meanwhile, cook the trenette in boiling salted water for about 7 minutes until just tender (*al dente*). Drain well.

place in a hot serving dish and stir in a little sauce, half the cheese and, if you wish, the remaining oil.

pour over the rest of the sauce just before serving, and sprinkle the chopped parsley over the top. Serve the remaining grated cheese separately.

Serves 4
Preparation time: *15–20 minutes*
Cooking time: *40 minutes*

clipboard: To remove the skin from a pepper, place the halved or quartered pepper under a moderately hot grill until the skin start to blacken and curl. At this pont scrape the skin off with a sharp knife.

Spaghetti *with sardines, anchovies and fennel*

Try this unusual pasta sauce — it's a special treat.

1 head fennel, quartered
8–10 tablespoons olive oil
2 garlic cloves, crushed
500 g/1 lb sardines
2 large onions, finely sliced
1 tablespoon sultanas
1 tablespoon pine nuts
6 anchovy fillets, chopped
2 tablespoons chopped parsley
150 ml/5 fl oz white wine or Fish Stock (see page 11)
500 g/1 lb spaghetti
white breadcrumbs, lightly browned
salt and freshly ground black pepper

cook the fennel in boiling salted water until almost tender. Drain well, reserving the cooking liquid. Chop the fennel coarsely.

heat 3 tablespoons oil in a pan and add the garlic. Cook gently until golden brown then add the sardines and cook gently for a further 10 minutes.

meanwhile, heat another 3 tablespoons of oil in a pan and cook the onions until they are soft and golden brown.

add the fennel, sultanas, pine nuts, anchovies, parsley and wine or fish stock. Season lightly. Cook over a moderate heat for 10 minutes.

cook the spaghetti in boiling salted water to which the fennel water has been added. Drain well and place half in an oven–to–table dish. Cover with half the sardines and a little of the onions and fennel.

repeat the layers and sprinkle breadcrumbs and a little oil over the top. Cook in a preheated oven at 200° C/400° F/ Gas Mark 6, for 20 minutes. Serve immediately, sprinkled with freshly ground black pepper.

Serves 4
Preparation time: *10 minutes*
Cooking time: *1 hour*
Oven temperature: *200° C/400° F/ Gas Mark 6*

clipboard: To prepare the sardines, bone them and remove the heads and tails. Cut each sardine into 2 or 3 pieces, depending on size, before cooking them.

Spaghetti alla Carbonara

This is a delightful way of using the familiar ingredients of egg and bacon in an authentic Italian dish.

500 g/1 lb spaghetti

8 rashers streaky bacon

2 tablespoons olive oil

3 eggs, beaten

3 tablespoons single cream

50 g/2 oz Parmesan cheese, grated

2 tablespoons chopped

fresh parsley, finely chopped, to garnish (optional)

salt and freshly ground black pepper

bring a pan of salted water to the boil, adding a little oil if wished to prevent the spaghetti sticking together.

when the water reaches a rolling boil, add the spaghetti to the pan and continue boiling until it is cooked through but still firm to the bite (*al dente*) Drain well.

while the spaghetti is cooking, chop the bacon rashers into small pieces and sauté in the olive oil in a large heavy-based saucepan until cooked and golden brown.

add the drained cooked spaghetti to the pan and gently stir in the beaten eggs, salt and freshly ground black pepper and cream.

stir very gently over a low heat until the egg starts to set.

toss the spaghetti mixture lightly with most of the Parmesan and serve immediately while still very hot, sprinkled with the remaining Parmesan and the chopped parsley, if used.

Serves:4
Preparation time: *5 minutes*
Cooking time: *15–20 minutes*

Spaghetti alla Bolognese

This is one of countless meat and vegetable sauces that are served with pasta. The beautiful city of Bologna is renowned for its fine pasta, and is the birthplace of several Italian classic recipes.

Meat sauce

4 tablespoons olive oil
1 onion, finely chopped
1 garlic clove, crushed
4 rashers streaky bacon, derinded and chopped
1 carrot, diced
1 celery stick, diced
500 g/1 lb lean minced beef
150 ml/¼ pint red wine
125 ml/4 fl oz milk
grated nutmeg
1 x 425 g/14 oz can chopped tomatoes
1 tablespoon sugar
1 teaspoon chopped fresh oregano
salt and freshly ground black pepper

500 g/1 lb spaghetti
1 teaspoon olive oil
freshly ground black pepper
50 g/2 oz Parmesan cheese, grated, to garnish (optional)

make the sauce: heat the oil in a saucepan or deep frying pan and sauté the onion, garlic, bacon, carrot and celery until soft and golden. Add the beef and cook, stirring occasionally, until browned.

add the red wine and bring to the boil. Reduce the heat slightly and cook over medium heat until most of the wine has evaporated. Season with salt and freshly ground black pepper.

add the milk and a little grated nutmeg, and stir well. Continue cooking until the milk has been absorbed by the meat mixture. Add the tomatoes, sugar and oregano. Reduce the heat to a bare simmer and cook, uncovered for 2–2½ hours until the sauce is reduced and richly coloured.

bring a large saucepan of salted water to the boil. Add the spaghetti and olive oil and cook until tender but firm to the bite (*al dente*). Drain well and season with freshly ground black pepper. Pour over the meat sauce and serve the Parmesan separately.

Serves 4
Preparation time: *10 minutes*
Cooking time: *2½–3 hours*

Spaghetti alle Vongole

This is the perfect recipe to cook when your fishmonger has fresh clams available. Try to get Venus or Palourde small clams if possible. Otherwise, fresh mussels or cockles can be used instead.

1 kg/2 lb fresh clams, scrubbed and cleaned (see clipboard below)
7 tablespoons water
7 tablespoons olive oil
1 garlic clove, peeled and sliced
425 g/14 oz tomatoes, skinned (see page 20) and mashed
425 g/14 oz spaghetti
salt and freshly ground black pepper
1 tablespoon chopped parsley

put the clams in a large pan with the water. Cook until the shells open, then remove the clams from the shells. Strain the cooking liquid and reserve for later.

heat the oil in a heavy pan, add the garlic and simmer gently for 5 minutes. Remove the garlic, then add the tomatoes and the reserved cooking liquid to the pasta. Stir and simmer for 20 minutes.

meanwhile, cook the spaghetti in plenty of boiling salted water until tender but firm to the bite (*al dente*). Drain thoroughly.

add the clams and parsley to the tomato sauce and heat thoroughly for 1 minute. Pile the spaghetti in a warmed serving dish, add the sauce and a pinch of pepper and fork gently to mix. Serve immediately.

Serves 4
Preparation time: *10 minutes*
Cooking time: *40 minutes*

clipboard: Fresh clams in their shells should be well scrubbed and washed before heating. To check if they are alive and well, tap the shell briskly — the clam should immediately respond by shutting tightly.

Tagliatelle
with tomato and basil sauce

A deceptively simple yet beautifully flavoured sauce to serve with pasta. Tomatoes, basil and olives are generously combined to produce a full, vibrant taste.

4 tablespoons olive oil
2 onions, chopped
2 garlic cloves, crushed
500 g/1 lb plum tomatoes, skinned (see page 20) and chopped
2 tablespoons tomato purée
1 teaspoon sugar
100 ml/3½ fl oz dry white wine
few ripe olives, pitted and quartered
handful of torn basil leaves
375 g/12 oz dried tagliatelle
salt and freshly ground black pepper
50 g/2 oz Parmesan cheese, shaved

heat 3 tablespoons of the olive oil in a large frying pan. Add the onions and garlic, and sauté gently over low heat until they are soft and slightly coloured. Stir the mixture occasionally.

add the tomatoes, tomato purée, sugar and wine, stirring well. Cook over gentle heat until the mixture is quite thick and reduced. Stir in the quartered olives and torn basil leaves, and season to taste with salt and plenty of freshly ground black pepper.

meanwhile, add the tagliatelle to a large pan of boiling salted water (to which a little oil has been added to prevent the pasta sticking together). Boil rapidly until the tagliatelle is tender but still firm to the bite (*al dente*).

drain the tagliatelle immediately, mixing in the remaining olive oil and a generous grinding of black pepper. Arrange the pasta on 4 serving plates and top with the tomato sauce, mixing it into the tagliatelle. Serve with large curls of shaved Parmesan.

Serves 4
Preparation time: *10 minutes*
Cooking time: *20 minutes*

Tagliatelle

with Borlotti beans and sage

Sage (or salvia) is widely used in Italian cooking, and imparts a pungent flavour. It combines very well with the beans, tomatoes, garlic and olive oil in this recipe.

3 tablespoons olive oil

75 g/3 oz smoked bacon, derinded and cubed

1 onion, finely chopped

5 sage leaves

1 x 250 g/8 oz can Borlotti beans

2 tablespoons Chicken Stock (see page 11)

¼ teaspoon flour

1 tablespoon tomato purée

2 tablespoons red wine

425 g/14 oz tagliatelle

2 tablespoons Parmesan cheese, grated

1 tablespoon pecorino cheese, grated

extra sage leaves to garnish (optional)

heat the oil in a large, heavy-based pan, add the bacon, onion and whole sage leaves. Cook over a medium heat until golden.

drain the Borlotti beans, rinse and drain again, then add to the pan.

heat the stock. Mix the flour and tomato purée in a small bowl; stir in the hot stock and the wine.

pour into the bean mixture, stir with a wooden spoon and simmer over a low heat until the sauce thickens.

cook the pasta in plenty of lightly salted boiling water until tender but firm to the bite (*al dente*).

remove the sage leaves from the sauce, taste and adjust the seasoning. Drain the pasta, mix with the sauce and put in a large heated serving dish. Add the Parmesan and pecorino, and serve hot, garnished with a few fresh sage leaves if liked.

Serves 4
Preparation time: *10 minutes*
Cooking time: *30 minutes*

Linguine
with mussels in tomato sauce

2.4 litres/4 pints mussels
3 tablespoons olive oil
1 onion, chopped
3 garlic cloves, crushed
750 g /1½ lb tomatoes, skinned (see page 20)
and chopped
500 g/1 lb linguine
salt and freshly ground black pepper
3 tablespoons fresh parsley, chopped

prepare the mussels as follows: cover them with cold water and discard any that open or float to the surface. Scrub the remaining mussels and remove the beards.

place in a large saucepan with 100 ml/3½ fl oz water, cover with a lid and cook over moderate heat until the mussels open, shaking the pan occasionally. Drain the mussels and remove the shells, leaving a few in their shells to garnish. Discard any that do not open.

heat the olive oil in a frying pan and add the onion and garlic. Sauté over medium heat until golden and tender.

add the chopped tomatoes, season, then cook gently over low heat until the mixture is thickened and reduced.

add the shelled mussels and mix gently into the tomato sauce. Simmer over low heat for 2–3 minutes or until the mussels are heated through.

cook the linguine in salted boiling water until it is tender but firm to the bite (*al dente*). Drain well and gently toss with the tomato and mussel sauce.

transfer to a serving dish or 4 warm plates. Sprinkle with chopped parsley and garnish with the reserved mussels.

Serves 4
Preparation time: *25 minutes*
Cooking time: *20 minutes*

Mushroom Ravioli

Ravioli is mostly shaped into crescents or circles when made at home, but whatever shape you choose, you'll enjoy the taste.

2 tablespoons olive oil
1 onion, finely chopped
1–2 garlic cloves, crushed
500 g/1 lb mushrooms, finely chopped
200 g/7 oz ricotta cheese
1 egg, beaten
2–3 tablespoons white breadcrumbs
1 x quantity egg pasta dough (see page 64)
75 g/3 oz butter
salt and freshly ground pepper
50 g/2 oz Parmesan cheese, grated

heat the oil, add the onion and garlic, and cook gently until soft and lightly coloured. Add the mushrooms and continue to cook gently until the mushrooms are soft and any liquid has evaporated.

remove from the heat, beat in the ricotta and egg and sufficient breadcrumbs to give a firm mixture. Season to taste.

roll out the pasta dough thinly and cut out 6 cm/2½ inch rounds. Place a portion of the mixture on each, brush around the edge of the dough with cold water, fold over and seal. Alternatively, cut out 2.5cm/1 inch square or round shapes, place the filling in the centre, brush around the edge of the dough with cold water, top with a matching shape and seal.

cook a few ravioli at a time for 4–5 minutes in boiling salted water. They are cooked when they rise to the surface. Remove with a draining spoon, drain well and place in a hot serving dish. Cover and keep hot until all the ravioli are cooked. Just before serving, heat the butter in a pan until it is a light golden brown, and pour immediately over the ravioli. Sprinkle a little of the Parmesan over the top and serve the rest separately. Serve hot with freshly ground black pepper.

Serves 4
Preparation time: *30 minutes*
Cooking time: *30 minutes*

Dry pasta

Riccioli

Tagliatelle

Penne

Farfalle

Spaghetti

Riccioli

Riccioli is similar in shape to the ready-stuffed pasta called cappaletti (which means 'little hats'). It is sold in dry form and has no stuffing. It is useful for holding morsels of food in the pasta sauce.

Farfalle

Farfalle is a delightful pasta which is made in different sized butterfly shapes — the pasta is pinched to form pretty butterflies/bow ties. It is very attractive served with a colourful sauce and garnished.

Tagliatelle

Tagliatelle is a very popular pasta which can be bought fresh or dried. It is very similar to fettucine but is slightly thinner and wider. It is served with all the classic pasta sauces, including bolognese.

Spaghetti

Spaghetti is probably the best known and most popular of all the pastas and can be bought fresh or dried. The long, thin rod-like pasta is generally associated with the famous bolognese sauce.

Penne

Penne is a hollow, quill-like pasta, which has diagonal ends on its tubes. It is a very popular, versatile pasta, and can be bought dried or fresh. Penne is boiled until just tender (*al dente*) and served with any of the classic pasta sauces.

Rigatoni

Swirls

Conchigl

Fiorelli

Casareccie

Conchiglie
Conchigle consists of small, pretty, dried shells of pasta. 'Conchiglie' means little conches or shells. As with other similarly-shaped pasta, it is often served with minced meat sauces. This is because the convenient little hollows in the shells tend to trap the meat inside and also retain the sauce.

Rigatoni
Rigatoni is a very popular pasta made in the form of ridged, hollow tubes. They are ideal for baking in a rich sauce. Alternatively they can be boiled until they are just tender (*al dente*) then tossed in a meaty pasta sauce. Like conchigle they are very good for retaining the meat and vegetable sauce.

Fiorelli
Fiorelli is a one of the few pasta shapes meant to resemble a flower. It is round and curly, and makes an attractive alternative to the more common pasta shapes. Fiorelli should be cooked until it is just tender (*al dente*) and served with the pasta sauce and garnish of your choice.

Swirls
This spiral shaped, dried pasta, should be cooked and served with a sauce of the cook's choice.

Casareccie
This small, twisted pasta originates from Sicily. It is made in long, thin strips, which are then twisted to create an interesting shape.

Baked Lasagne
with a savoury meat sauce

This baked lasagne dish is warming and tasty. It is substantial enough to serve on its own, piping hot, accompanied by a robust red wine and a fresh salad.

150–300 ml/¼–½ pint milk
450 ml/¾ pint béchamel sauce (see clipboard below)
salt and white pepper
1 x quantity Meat Sauce (see page 77), cooked for 20 minutes only
250 g/8 oz quick-cook dried green or white lasagne, or fresh pasta cut into thin 19 x 9 cm/7½ x 3½ inch sheets
375 g/12 oz Bel Paese or Fontina cheese, thinly sliced or grated
2–3 tablespoons Parmesan cheese, grated
sprig of fresh basil, to garnish

whisk sufficient milk into the béchamel sauce to make a thin creamy consistency. Check the seasoning.

butter an oven-to-table dish. Starting with a little meat sauce, layer the meat sauce, lasagne, béchamel sauce and Bel Paese or Fontina in the dish, ending with a layer of béchamel sauce.

sprinkle the Parmesan over the top and bake in a preheated oven at 180°C/350°F/Gas Mark 4 for 40–45 minutes. Serve hot, garnished with a sprig of fresh basil.

Serves 4
Preparation time: *15–20 minutes*
Cooking time: *40–45 minutes*
Oven Temperature: *180°C/350°F/Gas Mark 4*

clipboard: To make béchamel sauce: melt 40 g/1 1/2 oz butter and stir in 40 g/1 1/2 oz flour. Cook over gentle heat for 2–3 minutes, and gradually beat in 450 ml/3⁄4 pint milk, stirring constantly, until you have a thick, smooth, glossy sauce. Season with salt, pepper and a little nutmeg

Layered Pasta
with a Parmesan and meat sauce

A hearty meat sauce is blended with Parmesan and butter, resulting in a really wholesome baked lasagne.

1 x quantity Meat Sauce (see page 77)

Béchamel sauce
40 g/1½ oz butter
40 g/1½ flour
600 ml/1 pint milk
pinch of ground nutmeg
salt and freshly ground black pepper

250 g/8 oz quick-cook dried lasagne sheets, or freshly made lasagne
50 g/2 oz grated Parmesan cheese
15 g/½ oz butter

make the meat sauce, and simmer gently for at least 1 hour until it is time to assemble the lasagne.

make the béchamel sauce: melt the butter in a saucepan and stir in the flour. Cook over gentle heat, without browning, for 2–3 minutes and then gradually beat in the milk until you have a thick, smooth glossy sauce. Season with nutmeg, salt and pepper, and cook gently for 5–10 minutes.

put a little of the meat sauce in a buttered ovenproof dish and cover with a layer of lasagne and then another layer of meat sauce, topped with some béchamel sauce. Continue layering up in this way, ending with a layer of lasagne and a topping of béchamel.

sprinkle with grated Parmesan and then dot the top with butter. Bake in a preheated oven at 230°C/450°F/Gas Mark 8 for 30 minutes until the lasagne is golden brown.

Serves 4
Preparation time: *1¼ hours*
Cooking time: *30 minutes*
Oven temperature: *230°C/450°F/Gas Mark 8*

Penne

with a spicy sausage sauce

The best sausage to use in this recipe is a spicy Italian variety like salamelle. The fresh vegetables add a lovely, clean-flavoured taste to the pasta sauce.

3 tablespoons oil

25g/1 oz butter

½ onion, chopped

½ small shallot, chopped

1 small carrot, finely sliced

1 celery stalk, sliced

100 g/4 oz salamelle sausage, crumbled

½ small yellow sweet pepper, deseeded and diced

4 basil leaves, torn

50 ml/2 fl oz dry red wine

425 g/14 oz penne

2 tablespoons grated pecorino cheese

2 tablespoons grated Parmesan cheese

few whole basil leaves, to garnish

heat the oil and butter in a flameproof casserole, add the onion, shallot, carrot and celery, and cook over low heat for 4 minutes.

mix well then add the crumbled sausages, diced pepper and torn basil. Brown over medium heat for 3–4 minutes, and moisten with red wine.

cook the penne in lightly salted boiling water until tender but firm to the bite (*al dente*), and drain.

transfer the penne to a heated serving dish and pour on the sausage and vegetable sauce.

sprinkle with the cheeses and mix well before serving, garnished with whole basil leaves.

Serves 4
Preparation time: *10 minutes*
Cooking time: *10 minutes*

clipboard: Look around specialist Italian food stores or the delicatessen counters of supermarkets to find the spicy salamelle cooking sausage. If you can't get this, use continental sausage, or any good quality sausage.

Macaroni

with anchovies and garlic

This is how macaroni is prepared country-style in Italian households. The anchovies and olives provide a distinctly salty tang to the sauce.

2 anchovy fillets

a little milk

4 tablespoons oil

1 garlic clove

50 g/2 oz smoked bacon, derinded and diced

1 x 425 g/14 oz can plum tomatoes

50 g/2 oz pitted black olives, chopped

¼ teaspoon chopped oregano

375 g/12 oz macaroni

25 g/1 oz pecorino cheese, grated

salt and pepper

soak the anchovy fillets in a little milk to remove excess salt.

heat the oil in a small pan. Add the whole garlic clove and the drained anchovies. Cook over medium heat for a few minutes, then remove the garlic and add the bacon.

meanwhile, drain the tomatoes and cut into strips. When the bacon is crisp, add the tomatoes to the pan. Season with salt and pepper and leave to cook over low heat for about 20 minutes until a thick sauce has formed. Add the olives and oregano halfway through the cooking time.

cook the pasta in a large pan of lightly salted boiling water until tender but firm to the bite (*al dente*).

drain and transfer to a heated serving dish, then pour on the sauce and sprinkle with the grated pecorino cheese. Mix well before serving.

Serves 4
Preparation time: *10 minutes*
Cooking time: *30 minutes*

Roman Gnocchi
baked with Parmesan

Gnocchi are mouthwatering to eat, and great fun to prepare. They can be made either from potato or, as in this recipe, from semolina.

600 ml/1 pint milk
125 g/4 oz semolina
pinch of nutmeg
125 g/4 oz Gruyère cheese, grated
25–50 g/1–2 oz butter, melted
25–50 g/1–2 oz Parmesan cheese, grated
salt and white pepper

bring the milk to the boil. Remove from the heat and immediately add the semolina all at once. Beat well until smooth, season with a pinch of nutmeg and salt and pepper.

return to the heat, bring to the boil and cook for 5–7 minutes over moderate heat, beating vigorously all the time until the mixture leaves the sides of the pan. Beat in the Gruyère and check the seasoning.

turn out the mixture on to a buttered or oiled baking tray and spread into a sheet approximately 1–1.5 cm/½–¾ inch thick. Leave until cold, then refrigerate until completely firm.

cut the gnocchi into rounds with a 5–6 cm/2–2 ½ inch pastry cutter. Arrange, overlapping, in a buttered ovenproof dish. (Re-form any leftover mixture and cut out more rounds.) Pour the melted butter over the top and sprinkle with the Parmesan. Bake in a preheated oven at 220°C/425°F/Gas Mark 7 for 20–30 minutes until golden brown. Serve straight from the oven

Serves 4–6
Preparation time: *20–30 minutes, plus firming*
Cooking time: *30–40 minutes*
Oven temperature: *220°C/425°F/Gas Mark 7*

clipboard: To make this dish more substantial, cut 175 g/6 oz bacon rashers into strips. Fry them gently in a little oil and sprinkle over the gnocchi in the baking dish.

Potato Gnocchi
with tomato sauce

Tomato sauce
3 tablespoons olive oil
1 x 425 g/14oz can chopped tomatoes
1 teaspoon dried oregano
pinch sugar
salt and freshly ground black pepper

Gnocchi
750 g/1½ lb floury potatoes, peeled and cut into
even-sized pieces
175–200 g/6–7 oz plain flour
2 egg yolks, beaten
pinch of nutmeg
50–75 g/2–3 oz melted butter
50 g/2 oz Parmesan cheese, grated
salt and white pepper

make the tomato sauce: put all the ingredients in a pan and bring to the boil. Simmer briskly, uncovered, for 20–25 minutes, until the sauce is thick. Serve hot or cold as preferred.

cook the potatoes in boiling salted water until tender. Drain well and return to the heat for a few moments, shaking the pan all the time to dry out the potatoes. Sieve the potatoes through a vegetable mill or mash until quite smooth. Beat in most of the flour and the egg yolks, add the nutmeg, and mix until smooth.

turn out on to a floured board and knead in more flour, if necessary, to give a firm mixture. Roll out the potato mixture into sausage strips about 1 cm/½ inch in diameter and cut into 3 cm/1¼ inch pieces. Press the centre of each piece lightly between thumb and forefinger or with a fork to flatten them slightly.

cook the gnocchi, a few at a time, in a large pan of gently boiling water. They are cooked when they rise to the surface. Remove with a draining spoon and drain well.

place the cooked gnocchi in a hot buttered dish and keep hot until all the gnocchi are cooked. Before serving, pour the hot melted butter over the top. Sprinkle with a little Parmesan, and serve the rest separately with fresh tomato sauce.

Serves 4
Preparation time: *20–30 minutes*
Cooking time: *30–40 minutes*

Baked Macaroni
with fresh prawns

Béchamel sauce
25 g/1 oz butter
25 g/1 oz /flour
300 ml/½ pint milk
pinch of ground nutmeg
salt and freshly ground black pepper

90 g/3½ oz butter
175 g/6 oz button mushrooms, sliced
250 g/8 oz peeled prawns
2 tablespoons warmed brandy
50–75 g/2–3 oz Parmesan cheese, grated
250 g/8 oz short macaroni
sprigs of fresh basil, to garnish

make 300 ml/½ pint bechamel sauce (see page 90). Keep warm.

heat half the butter in a pan and cook the mushrooms until tender. Season to taste with salt and pepper.

add the prawns and heat through, then pour on the warmed brandy and set alight. When the flames have subsided, stir in half the cheese and check the seasoning.

meanwhile, cook the pasta in boiling salted water until just tender but still firm to the bite (*al dente*). Drain well. Check the seasoning of the béchamel sauce and add a pinch of nutmeg and the remaining cheese.

place one-third of the macaroni in a buttered oven-to-table dish and spread with half the mushroom mixture. Repeat the layers, ending with a layer of macaroni.

cover with the béchamel sauce. Heat the remaining butter in a pan and, when it is lightly coloured, pour it over the top. Bake in a preheated oven at 200°C/400°F/Gas Mark 6 for about 20 minutes until golden brown. Serve hot, garnished with fresh basil.

Serves 4
Preparation time: *15–20 minutes*
Cooking time: *35-40 minutes*
Oven temperature: *200°C/400°F/Gas Mark 6*

clipboard: For a more economical dish, you can use cod or smoked haddock which has been skinned, poached in water and broken into chunks with a fork.

Pork, Beef and Lamb

Loin of Pork

with juniper and bay leaves

2 tablespoons olive oil

1–1.25 kg/2–2½ lb boned loin of pork without rind, tied into a neat shape

1 tablespoon juniper berries, coarsely crushed

2 cloves

10 bay leaves, fresh if possible, plus a sprig to garnish

2 large onions, chopped

300 ml/½ pint dry white wine

150–450 ml/¼–¾ pint Chicken Stock (see page 11)

salt and freshly ground black pepper

heat the olive oil in a heavy-based pan or flameproof casserole, just large enough to hold the meat. Brown the meat on all sides.

add the juniper berries, cloves, bay leaves and onions, and stir in to the oil.

season to taste with salt and pepper and pour on the white wine.

cover with a piece of greaseproof paper and a tight-fitting lid and cook very gently for 1½ hours or until tender.

avoid removing the lid too often but check once or twice while the meat is cooking, adding a little stock if necessary.

remove the meat from the pan, and place on a serving dish. Cover and keep hot.

add sufficient stock to the pan to absorb all the browned residue in the stock. Bring to the boil, check the seasoning, and strain the liquid. If liked, pour a little over the meat, serving the rest separately. Serve hot, garnished with a fresh bay sprig.

Serves 4–6
Preparation time: *10 minutes*
Cooking time: *1½–2 hours*

clipboard: If you prefer, cook the meat in a preheated moderate oven at 180°C/350°F/Gas Mark 4. Take care that the greaseproof paper does not hang over the sides of the pan by more than 1 cm/½ inch. Too much paper could be a fire hazard, especially near a gas flame.

Milanese Stew
with pork loin and sausages

This hearty casserole is full of juicy, meaty flavour. Eat it with plenty of crusty bread to mop up the sauce.

300 g/10 oz pork rind
25 g/1 oz butter
3–4 tablespoons olive oil
2 large onions, sliced
2 large carrots, sliced
2 sticks celery, chopped
625 g/1¼ lb boneless pork, diced
150 ml/¼ pint dry white wine
1.5 litres/2½ pints Chicken Stock (see page 11)
250 g/8 oz Italian pork sausage or Continental sausage, cut into 2.5 cm/1 inch slices
750 g/1½ lb Savoy cabbage, trimmed and shredded
salt and pepper

place the pork rind in a pan, cover with water and salt lightly. Bring to the boil and cook for 10 minutes. Drain and cut the rind into 5 cm x 1 cm/ 2 inch x ½ inch strips.

heat the butter and half the oil in another pan. Cook the onion until soft but without colour, then add the carrots and celery, and cook for about 5 minutes, stirring frequently.

take the vegetables from the pan. Heat the remaining oil and cook the pork until it is well sealed. Return the vegetables and pork rind to the pan and pour on the white wine and stock. Season to taste with salt and pepper.

simmer gently for 1½–2 hours until the meat is almost tender. Add the sausage and cabbage, and continue cooking for a further 25–30 minutes. Taste and adjust the seasoning, and transfer to a serving dish. Serve hot.

Serves 4–6
Preparation time: *20–25 minutes*
Cooking time: *2–2½ hours*

clipboard: Make this dish the day before you eat it, as standing improves the flavour. Refrigerate it when cold and reheat for 40 minutes over a low heat the following day.

Venetian Beef

in an aromatic, spiced marinade

Gentle simmering in wine and marsala adds complex flavours to this exquisite dish.

300 ml/10 fl oz red wine vinegar
1 garlic clove, chopped
2 cloves
pinch of cinnamon
2 carrots, chopped
2 sticks celery, chopped
1 sprig each rosemary and thyme
75 g/3 oz butter
1.5 x 1.75 kg/3–3½ lb joint topside or top rump
1 large onion, chopped
300 ml/10 fl oz dry white wine
300 ml/10 fl oz Marsala
salt and freshly ground pepper
fresh herbs, to garnish

mix together the vinegar, garlic, cloves, cinnamon, carrots, celery and herbs, and season well. Place the meat in a deep dish and pour over the marinade. Cover and refrigerate for 12 hours, turning the meat frequently.

drain the meat and vegetables and dry them on absorbent kitchen paper. Discard the liquid.

heat the butter in a heavy-based pan and cook the onion, carrots and celery until soft. Remove the vegetables from the pan and add the meat. Brown well on all sides. Return the vegetables to the pan with the wine, Marsala, and salt and pepper to taste. Cover the pan with a piece of greaseproof paper and a tight-fitting lid, and cook over gentle heat for 2–2½ hours until the meat is tender.

cut the meat into thick slices and arrange on a hot dish. Check the seasoning and strain the sauce over the meat. Sprinkle with black pepper, and garnish with fresh herbs.

Serves 6–8
Preparation time: *25–30 minutes, plus marinating*
Cooking time: *2¼–2¾ hours*

clipboard: To prepare the meat, remove all fat and retie the joint so that it makes a neat shape. This dish is traditionally eaten with polenta, a staple food of northern Italy (see page 180).

Bistecche *topped with a spicy pizzaiolo sauce*

This dish gets its name because the beef steak is cooked like pizza, with a topping of tomatoes, garlic and oregano. You can also cook pork chops in the same manner.

75 ml/3 fl oz olive oil
1–2 garlic cloves, crushed
500 g/1 lb tomatoes, peeled and chopped, or
1 x 425 g/14 oz can chopped tomatoes
1 teaspoon fresh chopped oregano or ½ teaspoon dried oregano
4 x 250 g/8 oz beef steaks, thinly cut, trimmed of all fat
salt and pepper

heat three-quarters of the oil in a pan and cook the garlic gently until golden brown. Add the tomatoes, and season lightly with salt, pepper and oregano.

bring to the boil and simmer for 10–15 minutes until the sauce thickens slightly. Canned tomatoes will take longer than fresh ones.

meanwhile, heat the remaining oil in a frying pan and quickly brown the meat on both sides. Pour over the sauce and continue cooking very gently for 10–15 minutes or until the meat is tender. If necessary, add a little water to prevent the sauce reducing too much.

arrange the steaks on hot individual plates or a serving dish and pour the sauce over. Serve immediately.

Serves 4
Preparation time: *15–20 minutes*
Cooking time: *25–35 minutes*

Beef Olives

stuffed with cheese, ham and basil

This is both elegant and simple — and makes a perfect main course for a dinner party

1 kg/2 lb beef topside
125 g/4 oz pecorino cheese, grated
2 slices raw ham (prosciutto crudo), chopped
3 garlic cloves, crushed
3 tablespoons chopped fresh parsley
1 tablespoon chopped fresh basil
3 tablespoons olive oil
salt and freshly ground black pepper

Tomato sauce

1 onion, chopped
2 garlic cloves, crushed
1 kg/2 lb tomatoes, skinned (see page 20) and chopped
1 tablespoon tomato purée
125 ml/4 fl oz red wine
salt and freshly ground black pepper

cut the beef into thin slices and place between 2 sheets of greaseproof paper. Flatten the slices of beef with a rolling pin and then season with salt and pepper.

make the stuffing: put the grated pecorino cheese in a bowl with the chopped ham, garlic, parsley and basil.

mix together well and spread a little of this mixture on each piece of beef. Roll up, folding in the sides, and tie securely with cotton or fine string.

heat the olive oil in a large saucepan and gently fry the beef olives until they are slightly brown all over, turning as necessary. Remove from the pan and keep warm.

make the sauce: add the onion and garlic to the oil in the pan and sauté until soft. Add the tomatoes, tomato purée, wine and seasoning. Bring to the boil and then add the beef olives..

cover and simmer gently for 1½–2 hours or until tender. Remove the string from the beef olives and serve them hot. Serve the sauce separately.

Serves 6
Preparation time: *20 minutes*
Cooking time: *1½–2¼ hours*

Braised Beef
in red wine with rosemary

The long, slow cooking method in this recipe is an ideal way to bring out the flavours of any joint of beef suitable for braising.

1.5 kg/3 lb joint of beef – topside
or rolled silverside
1 onion, sliced
1 carrot, sliced
1 celery stick, sliced
2 garlic cloves, crushed
2 bay leaves
6 peppercorns
600 ml/1 pint red wine such as Barolo
25 g/1 oz bacon fat or dripping
1 onion, finely chopped
1 sprig of rosemary
salt and freshly ground pepper

put the meat in a deep bowl. Add the sliced onion, carrot, celery, garlic, bay leaves, peppercorns and red wine. Cover the bowl and place in the refrigerator to marinate for 24 hours, turning the beef several times. Lift the meat out of the marinade and dry it carefully. Reserve the marinade.

heat the bacon fat or dripping in a large flameproof casserole and sauté the chopped onion over low heat for about 5 minutes or until it is soft and golden. Put in the beef, increase the heat and brown quickly on all sides.

strain the reserved marinade into the casserole and bring to the boil. Add the rosemary sprig and season with salt and pepper.

lower the heat, cover tightly and simmer very gently for at least 3 hours or until the meat is tender. Turn the meat once halfway through cooking.

transfer the meat to a carving dish or board and slice fairly thickly. Arrange the slices on a warm serving dish. If the sauce is too thin, reduce a little by rapid boiling.

remove the rosemary and pour the sauce over the meat. Serve immediately with puréed potatoes and carrots.

Serves 6
Preparation time: *5 minutes, plus 24 hours marinating time*
Cooking time: *3¼ hours*

Mountain Lamb
in wine and mushrooms

Shepherds in the mountains of Basilicata tend their flocks of sheep as they have done for hundreds of years. This is a traditional way of cooking lamb, using fresh mushrooms from the meadows.

3 tablespoons olive oil
1 kg/2 lb boned shoulder or leg of lamb, cut into serving pieces (see clipboard below)
500 g/1 lb mushrooms,
125 ml/4 fl oz dry white wine
salt and freshly ground black pepper

heat the oil in a flameproof casserole, add the meat and fry over moderate heat until browned on all sides.

add the mushrooms, wine and enough water to just cover the meat. Season with salt and pepper to taste.

cover and cook in a preheated moderately hot oven at 190°C/375°F/Gas Mark 5 for 1 hour or until the meat is tender, stirring occasionally.

serve hot, with steamed spinach and slices of polenta, if liked.

Serves 4
Preparation time: *10 minutes*
Cooking time: *1 hour 15 minutes*
Oven temperature: *190°C/375°F/Gas Mark 5*

clipboard: This is a good way to use an economical joint like shoulder of lamb. Buy the leanest piece you can find, however, as it is rather fatty. Your butcher will remove the bone on request.

Braised Lamb
with celery and onions

This is another delicious recipe for mountain lamb, here braised with fresh celery and onions, keeping the flavour of the meat pure and simple.

3 tablespoons olive oil
2 celery sticks, chopped
375 g/12 oz pickling onions
1 kg/2 lb boned leg or shoulder of lamb, cut into serving pieces
2–3 rosemary sprigs, cut into pieces
2 bay leaves
450 ml/¾ pint Chicken Stock (see page 11)
salt and freshly ground black pepper

heat the oil in a flameproof casserole, add the celery and onions and fry gently for 5 minutes.

add the meat, half the rosemary, the bay leaves and salt and pepper to taste. Fry over moderate heat until the meat is browned on all sides.

stir in the stock and just enough water to cover the meat.

cover and simmer for 1 hour or until the meat is tender. Discard the herbs before serving.

serve hot, garnished with the remaining rosemary.

Serves 4
Preparation time: *20 minutes*
Cooking time: *1½ hours*

Sardinian Lamb
with fennel and tomatoes

*Large flocks of sheep graze the high mountains
on the island of Sardinia, where lamb is very plentiful.
This recipe has fennel as a main ingredient,
which gives a pungent, aromatic flavour to the sauce.*

5 tablespoons olive oil
1 kg/2 lb boned leg of lamb, cut into serving pieces
1 onion, peeled and chopped
400 g/14 oz tomatoes, skinned (see page 20) and mashed
675g/1½ lb fennel, quartered
salt and freshly ground black pepper

heat the oil in a flameproof casserole, add the meat and fry over moderate heat until lightly browned on all sides.

stir in the onion and fry for a further 5 minutes. Add the tomatoes and salt and pepper to taste.

lower the heat, cover and simmer for 40 minutes, adding a little water if the casserole becomes too dry during cooking.

meanwhile, cook the fennel in boiling salted water for 20 minutes. Drain and reserve 200 ml/7 fl oz of the cooking liquid.

add the fennel and the reserved cooking liquid to the casserole, and continue cooking for about 20 minutes until the meat is tender. The casserole should be fairly dry. Serve hot, sprinkled with black pepper.

Serves 4
Preparation time: *20 minutes*
Cooking time: *1–1½ hours*

Scallopine alla Milanese

Veal is extremely popular in Italy, and is a traditional favourite on every Italian restaurant menu. This recipe is easy and quick to cook at home.

4 veal escalopes, each weighing 125 g/4 oz
1–2 eggs, beaten
dried breadcrumbs for coating
75 g/3 oz butter
salt and freshly ground black pepper

Garnish
lemon twists
parsley sprigs, chopped

beat the veal lightly with a mallet to flatten.

dip into the beaten egg and coat with breadcrumbs.

melt the butter in a large frying pan and fry the veal for 2–3 minutes on each side until tender and golden brown.

transfer the cooked veal to a warmed serving dish and sprinkle with salt and pepper to taste.

garnish with lemon twists and chopped parsley and serve immediately with fresh green beans.

Serves 4
Preparation time: *10 minutes*
Cooking time: *8–10 minutes*

Scallopine alla Bolognese

The Bolognese style of cooking veal escalopes adds the rich, melting flavours of marsala wine, cheese and Parma ham to the delicate meat.

8 small veal escalopes, weighing about 75 g/3 oz each
flour for coating
75 g/3 oz butter
8 thin slices Parma ham
8 thin slices Gruyère or Emmenthal cheese
3 tablespoons Marsala
3 tablespoons Chicken Stock (see page 11)
salt and freshly ground black pepper

beat the escalopes lightly with a rolling pin to thin them out. Sprinkle each one with a little salt and coat them with flour.

melt the butter in a large frying pan, and when foaming, sauté the escalopes for about 6–8 minutes on both sides until they are browned and cooked. Arrange them side-by-side in a buttered ovenproof dish.

cover each escalope with a slice of ham and then top with a slice of cheese. Leave them in a warm place while you deglaze the pan.

add the Marsala and stock to the buttery juices in the pan and season with pepper. Bring to the boil, scraping the bottom of the pan with a wooden spoon and stirring well. Spoon the sauce around the escalopes in the ovenproof dish and season with pepper. Place in a preheated oven at 230°C/450°F/Gas Mark 8, or under the grill for 5–10 minutes until the cheese has melted. Add a few grinds of black pepper and serve hot.

Serves 4
Preparation time: *10 minutes*
Cooking time: *14–20 minutes*
Oven temperature: *230°C/450°F/Gas Mark 8*

Veal Escalopes
and sage with Parma ham

This dish appears on restaurant menus as Saltimbocca alla Romana, and is a perfect example of the Italian genius for combining ingredients which make a happy marriage of flavour and texture.

8 small veal escalopes, weighing about 50 g/2 oz each
8 paper thin slices of Parma ham
8 fresh sage leaves
75g/3 oz butter
75 ml/3 fl oz Marsala or dry white wine
salt
fresh sage leaves, to garnish

beat the escalopes out thinly and trim the slices of ham to about the same size as the escalopes.

sprinkle each escalope with a pinch of salt and place a sage leaf on top. Cover each escalope with a slice of ham and secure with a cocktail stick soaked previously in cold water. Do not roll them up.

heat 50 g/2 oz of the butter in a large frying pan and, when foaming, add the escalopes and sauté briskly on both sides, removing the cocktail stick before turning. Cook until golden – about 6–8 minutes. Remove from the pan and keep warm.

add the Marsala or white wine to the buttery juices left in the pan. Bring to the boil, scraping the bottom of the pan with a wooden spoon and stirring well. Stir in the remaining butter and spoon the sauce over the escalopes. Garnish with fresh sage leaves.

Serves 4
Preparation time: *10 minutes*
Cooking time: *12–15 minutes*

Milanese Veal
stuffed with prosciutto and Parmesan

This is a clever way of making the meat go further, while adding extra flavours.

12 small thin slices of veal
6 fresh sage leaves
2 rashers streaky bacon
50 g/2 oz butter
4 tablespoons Marsala
4 tablespoons dry white wine
3 fresh sage leaves, roughly chopped

Filling
50 g/2 oz raw smoked ham (prosciutto crudo), chopped
1 chicken liver, finely chopped
25 g/1 oz fresh white breadcrumbs
2 tablespoons freshly grated Parmesan cheese
1 teaspoon finely chopped parsley
1 egg, beaten
¼ teaspoon freshly grated nutmeg
salt and freshly ground black pepper

make the filling: put the chopped ham, chicken liver, breadcrumbs, Parmesan and parsley in a bowl. Bind together with the beaten egg and season to taste with nutmeg, salt and pepper.

beat the slices of veal flat with a rolling pin. Put some of the filling on each slice of veal and roll it up. Thread 2 veal rolls on to each of 6 short wooden skewers soaked previously in cold water, together with a sage leaf. Cut each bacon rasher into 3 pieces and then thread one on to each skewer.

heat the butter in a frying pan and then sauté the veal rolls until they are evenly cooked and golden brown, turning occasionally. Remove the veal rolls from the pan and keep warm while you make the sauce.

add the Marsala and wine to the buttery pan juice and bring to the boil, scraping the bottom of the pan clean with a wooden spoon. Add the chopped sage and simmer for 3–5 minutes until reduced slightly. Pour the sauce over the veal rolls and serve immediately.

Serves 4–6
Preparation time: *15 minutes*
Cooking time: *12–15 minutes*

Salamelle Sausage
with broccoli and garlic

The hearty flavours of deliciously spicy, pungent salamelle sausages make a perfect match with the robust taste of fresh green broccoli.

25 g/1 oz dripping or lard
2 garlic cloves, chopped
1 piece of canned pimento
500 g/1 lb salamelle or Continental sausages
750 g/1½ lb broccoli
salt and freshly ground black pepper

melt the dripping or lard in a flameproof casserole, add the garlic and fry gently until browned.

stir in the pimento, sausages and salt and pepper to taste.

cover and bake in a preheated moderate oven at 190°C/375°F/Gas Mark 5 for about 45 minutes until the sausages are cooked.

meanwhile, cook the broccoli in boiling salted water for 15 minutes until tender. Drain and place in a warmed serving dish.

add the sausages, toss well and serve immediately.

Serves 4
Preparation time: *5–10 minutes*
Cooking time: *1 hour*
Oven temperature: *190°C/375°F/Gas Mark 5*

clipboard: *Salamelle* is a traditional Italian cooking sausage, sold in small links, and is available from Italian food stores or at supermarket delicatessen counters. It is made in several varieties, some of which are hot and peppery.

Calves' Liver
cooked Venetian-style

This is the speciality of one of Italy's most beautiful cities. The delicate combination of wafer-thin, prime meat with onions and parsley is a world away from "liver and onions".

3–4 tablespoons olive oil
25 g/1 oz butter
500 g/1 lb onions, sliced
1 tablespoon chopped parsley, plus extra to garnish
500 g/1 lb calves' liver, sliced very thinly
4 tablespoons Beef Stock (see page 10)
salt and freshly ground black pepper
flat-leaf parsley, to garnish

heat the oil and butter in a frying pan, add the onions and parsley and cook gently for 2–3 minutes.

add the liver, increase the heat and stir in the stock.

cook the liver for 5 minutes, then remove from the heat and add salt and pepper to taste.

serve immediately on a bed of mashed potatoes, topped with sautéed mushrooms and garnished with chopped parsley.

Serves 4
Preparation time: *5 minutes*
Cooking time: *10–15 minutes*

Poultry
and Game

Chicken Marengo

Prawns, eggs and fried croûtons give this braised chicken dish extra substance and flavour

8–10 tablespoons olive oil

1 x 1.5 kg/3 lb chicken, jointed

350 g/12 oz ripe tomatoes, skinned (see page 20) deseeded and chopped

2 garlic cloves, crushed

300 ml/½ pint dry white wine

2 x 5 mm/¼ inch slices of bread, crusts removed and cut into triangles

4–6 large prawns

4–6 eggs

salt and freshly ground black pepper

2 tablespoons chopped parsley, to garnish

heat 2–3 tablespoons of oil in a flameproof casserole and fry the chicken pieces until golden brown on all sides. Remove from the pan. Pour some of the oil from the pan, if necessary, and add the tomatoes, garlic and white wine. Season to taste and mix well.

return the chicken to the pan, bring to the boil and cook in a preheated oven at 190°C/375°F/Gas Mark 5 for 35–45 minutes or until it is tender.

meanwhile, heat another 2–3 tablespoons of oil in a frying pan and fry the bread until golden brown on all sides. Remove from the pan and keep hot. Fry the prawns for 2–3 minutes until cooked through. Keep hot. Heat another 2–3 tablespoons of olive oil in a clean pan and fry the eggs.

when the chicken is cooked, arrange it on a hot serving dish. If necessary, boil the sauce to reduce it to a thin coating consistency. Check the seasoning and pour over the chicken.

arrange the prawns, eggs and fried croûtons around the sides of the dish. Sprinkle with parsley before serving. Serve hot.

Serves 4–6
Preparation time: *30–40 minutes*
Cooking time: *50–55 minutes*
Oven temperature: *190°C/375°F/Gas Mark 5*

clipboard: This dish is based on one created by Napoleon's chef after the Battle of Marengo using what ingredients he could find near the battlefield. To emulate the deep-fried eggs of the original recipe, fry the eggs on both sides.

Pollo alla Cacciatore

This is a typical 'hunter's style' of cooking which gives the chicken a hearty, rustic flavour.

4 tablespoons olive oil

4 slices pancetta or unsmoked bacon, chopped

1 large chicken, about 1.5 kg/3 lb, cut into 4 portions

2 garlic cloves, crushed

2 red onions, roughly chopped

500 g/1 lb tomatoes, skinned (see page 20) and chopped

250 g/8 oz mushrooms, sliced

1 sprig of rosemary

1 bay leaf

150 ml/¼ pint dry white wine

300 ml/½ pint Chicken Stock (see page 111)

salt and freshly ground black pepper

1 tablespoon chopped parsley, to garnish

heat the oil in a large frying pan and fry the pancetta or bacon for 2–3 minutes until browned.

stir occasionally to prevent the pancetta or bacon from sticking. Remove and keep warm.

put the chicken portions in the pan and sauté in the oil, turning occasionally, until they are golden brown all over.

remove the chicken from the pan and keep warm. Add the garlic, onions, tomatoes and mushrooms and cook gently over low heat for 5 minutes, stirring occasionally. Return the chicken to the frying pan.

add the herbs, then pour in the wine and chicken stock. Simmer gently for about 1 hour until the chicken is tender and the sauce reduced. Season to taste with salt and pepper.

Serves 4
Preparation time: *15 minutes*
Cooking time: *1¼ hours*

Pan-fried chicken

A quick and simple dish that relies on the quality of its ingredients. Serve it with a tossed green salad or a fresh green vegetable such as mangetouts, French beans or broccoli.

3 tablespoons olive oil

1 tablespoon butter

4 chicken breasts, skinned

175 ml/6 fl oz dry white wine

4-6 fresh sage leaves, roughly chopped

3 tablespoons balsamic vinegar

salt and freshly ground black pepper

fresh sage leaves, to garnish

heat the oil and butter in a large non-stick frying pan until foaming. Add the chicken and cook over low to moderate heat for 5-7 minutes until golden brown on both sides, turning once.

pour the wine over the chicken and sprinkle over the chopped sage and salt and pepper to taste. Cover and cook over low heat for 15 minutes, spooning the sauce over the chicken from time to time and turning the chicken halfway through cooking.

remove the chicken to warmed dinner plates and keep warm. Add the balsamic vinegar to the pan juices, increase the heat to high and stir until the juices are reduced. Spoon the juices over the chicken, garnish with sage sprigs and serve immediately.

Serves 4

Preparation time: *5 minutes*

Cooking time: *25–30 minutes*

clipboard: Chicken breasts on the bone have the most tender, moist meat, and they are less likely to dry out during cooking. They are available in some good supermarkets. Boneless chicken breasts are easier to obtain and they can be used for this dish, but take care to baste them frequently and not to overcook them — the total cooking time should be only 15 minutes.

Baby Chickens
spatchcocked and barbecued

2 poussins, spatchcocked, (see clipboard)
125 ml/4 fl oz olive oil
6 tablespoons lemon juice
2 tablespoons mixed peppercorns, crushed coarsely
in a mortar and pestle
coarse sea or rock salt
lemon wedges, to serve

put the poussins in a non-metallic dish, and slash them all over with the point of a small sharp knife.

whisk together the oil, lemon juice and crushed peppercorns, and brush all over the poussins, working the marinade into the cuts in the meat. Cover and leave to marinate for at least 4 hours, preferably overnight in the refrigerator.

prepare the barbecue and let it burn until the flames have died down and the coals have turned grey. Sprinkle the skin side of the poussins with salt, then place them skin-side down on the barbecue grill. Cook for 15 minutes, then turn the poussins over and cook for a further 10 minutes.

remove the poussins from the barbecue grill and cut each bird in half lengthways with poultry shears. Serve hot, warm or cold, with lemon wedges for squeezing.

Serves 4
Preparation time: *10 minutes*, plus marinating
Cooking time: *25 minutes*

clipboard: Spatchcocking is simple: with the bird breast-side down, cut along each side of the backbone with poultry shears. Discard the backbone, or use in the stockpot. Put the bird breast-side up on a board and press hard with the heels of your hand on the breastbone to break it. To keep the bird flat during cooking, push 2 metal skewers through the bird, one through the wings with the breast in between, the other through the thighs.

Wild Boar
with sausage and polenta

For the Marinade
750 ml/1 1/4 pints red wine
1 onion, roughly chopped
1 carrot, roughly chopped
1 celery stick, roughly chopped
1 bay leaf
1 sprig each of sage and rosemary
1 tablespoon crushed black peppercorns
1 tablespoon crushed juniper berries

1.5 kg/3 lb boneless wild boar, cut into large cubes
6 tablespoons olive oil
1 onion, finely chopped
1 carrot, finely chopped
1 celery stick, finely chopped
1 garlic clove, crushed
2 salamelle sausages cut into chunks
600 ml/1 pint Beef Stock (see page10)
300 ml/1/2 pint red wine
125 ml/4 fl oz passata
2 tablespoons chopped flat-leaf parsley
1 teaspoon chopped fresh sage
1 teaspoon chopped fresh thyme
salt and freshly ground black pepper
fresh sage leaves, to garnish

For the polenta
750 ml/1 1/4 pints water
250 ml/8 fl oz milk
250 g/8 oz quick-cook polenta
50 g/2 oz butter
1 teaspoon salt

start by making the marinade for the meat. Put all the ingredients for the marinade in a saucepan and bring to the boil. Pour into a large bowl, leave to cool, then add the meat. Cover and marinate in the refrigerator overnight. The next day, remove the meat from the marinade with a slotted spoon and pat dry with kitchen paper. Discard the marinade.

heat the oil in a flameproof casserole, add the onion, carrot, celery and garlic and cook gently, stirring frequently, for about 5 minutes until softened but not coloured.

add the meat and sausages and cook over a medium heat, stirring, until browned on all sides, then add the stock, wine and passata and bring to the boil. Lower the heat and add the herbs and salt and pepper to taste, cover and simmer very gently for 2 hours or until the meat is tender.

cook the polenta: bring the water to the boil in a large heavy saucepan, add 1 teaspoon salt, then sprinkle in the polenta in a thin, steady stream, stirring all the time with a wooden spoon. Cook over a low heat, stirring constantly, for 8 minutes or according to the packet instructions. Remove from the heat and beat in the butter until melted.

divide the polenta between 4 warmed dinner plates, then spoon the stew over and around. Garnish with sage leaves and serve immediately.

Serves 4
Preparation time: *30 minutes*, plus marinating
Cooking time: *2–2½ hours*

clipboard: Wild boar can be bought at specialist butchers and game dealers. If you find it difficult to obtain, substitute venison.

Chicken

with tomatoes and pimento

Colourful, warming and easy-to-prepare, this dish could be served with boiled potatoes and a mixed salad.

3–4 tablespoons olive oil
1 small onion, sliced
2 garlic cloves, crushed
1 x 1.25 kg/2½ lb oven ready chicken, cut into serving pieces
1 small piece canned pimento, chopped
4 medium tomatoes
1 tablespoon tomato purée
3–4 tablespoons dry white wine
few rosemary sprigs
6–8 tablespoons Chicken Stock (see page 11)
salt and freshly ground black pepper

heat the oil in a flameproof casserole, add the onion and garlic and fry gently for 15 minutes.

add the chicken pieces with the pimento, tomatoes and salt and pepper to taste, and fry, turning, over moderate heat until evenly browned on all sides.

mix the tomato purée with a little lukewarm water, then stir into the casserole with the wine.

lower the heat, cover and continue cooking gently for 30 minutes.

chop one of the rosemary sprigs and sprinkle over the chicken.

cook for a further 30 minutes or until the chicken is tender, adding a little of the stock occasionally to moisten.

serve hot, garnished with the remaining rosemary.

Serves 4
Preparation time: *20–30 minutes*
Cooking time: *1½ hours*

Roast Chicken
with egg and cheese stuffing

A triumph of Italian taste and invention, this is a refreshingly different way of cooking roast chicken.

25 g/1 oz butter
1 x 1.5 kg/3 lb oven-ready chicken with giblets
150 g/5 oz dried breadcrumbs
3 tomatoes, skinned (see page 20) and chopped
1 egg, beaten
100 g/4 oz pecorino cheese, grated
7 tablespoons milk
4 tablespoons cream
1 hard-boiled egg
4 tablespoons olive oil
salt and freshly ground black pepper

melt the butter in a heavy-based pan, chop the chicken giblets and add to the pan. Fry gently for 10 minutes.

add the breadcrumbs and fry until browned, then add the tomatoes and simmer for 10 minutes. Remove from the heat and leave to cool.

add the egg to the mixture with the cheese, milk, cream and salt and pepper to taste.

mix thoroughly. Stuff the chicken with this mixture, putting the hard-boiled egg in the centre. Sew the opening securely with trussing thread or clean string.

place the chicken in an oiled roasting tin, pour over the olive oil, and sprinkle with salt and pepper to taste.

roast in a preheated, moderately hot oven at 200°C/400°F/Gas Mark 6 for 1½ hours or until the chicken is tender. Serve immediately.

Serves 6
Preparation time: *30 minutes*
Cooking time: *1½-2 hours*
Oven temperature: *200°C/400°F/Gas Mark 6*

Guinea Fowl
sautéed in butter with tomatoes

Once a game bird related to the pheasant, the guinea fowl has long been reared domestically. Its flesh has a distinctive flavour and is also good roasted or casseroled.

1 x 1.5 kg/3–3½ lb guinea fowl, jointed (see clipboard)
50 g/2 oz butter
2–3 tablespoons olive oil
450 g/1 lb tomatoes, skinned (see page 20), deseeded and sliced or 1 x 400 g/14 oz can tomatoes, drained, deseeded and sliced
salt and pepper
1 tablespoon chopped parsley, to garnish

season the guinea fowl with salt and pepper. Heat the butter and oil in a flameproof casserole and brown the pieces of guinea fowl well on all sides over a good heat.

lower the heat, cover with a tight-fitting lid and cook over a gentle heat, turning the pieces of guinea fowl from time to time for 25–35 minutes or until the bird is tender.

drain off most of the fat from the pan and add the tomatoes. Cook until they thicken slightly and season to taste. Pour into a serving dish, sprinkle over the parsley and serve hot with small roast potatoes.

Serves 4
Preparation time: *15–20 minutes*
Cooking time: *40–45 minutes*

clipboard: To joint the guinea fowl, place it on a board, breast uppermost, and cut through the skin between the body and the leg. Press the whole leg (the thigh and drumstick) outwards) to break the joint. Cut through any flesh, sinew or skin holding the leg to the carcass. Cut through the joint between the thigh and the drumstick. Repeat on the other side. Trim the first two joints away from the wing. Cut the breast away from the wing and break the wing joint in the same way as the leg. Cut through this joint. Cut the breast into two pieces.

Turkey Breasts
with Parmesan, egg and spinach

2 eggs
50 g/2 oz Parmesan cheese, grated
3–4 tablespoons olive oil
300 g/10 oz spinach, chopped
pinch of nutmeg
4 rashers lean rindless streaky bacon
2 x 250–300 g/8–10 oz turkey breast fillets
25 g/1 oz butter
300 ml/10 fl oz dry white wine
½ teaspoon chopped rosemary
salt and freshly ground black pepper

whisk one of the eggs with half the Parmesan and season well. Heat a scant tablespoon of oil in a 15 cm/6 inch frying pan. Cook until golden brown, then turn over and cook on the reverse side. Make another omelette.

heat a tablespoon of oil in another pan, and cook the spinach over a moderate heat until it softens. Season with nutmeg, salt and pepper.

place an omelette, half the spinach and 2 rashers of streaky bacon on each prepared turkey fillet, Roll up towards the pointed end and secure with cocktail sticks, previously soaked in cold water, and string.

melt the butter and a tablespoon of oil in a flameproof casserole and brown the turkey on all sides. Pour on the wine, add the rosemary, season, cover and cook in a preheated oven at 180°C/350°F/Gas Mark 4 for 1–1¼ hours until the turkey is tender. Take the turkey fillets from the pan and remove the cocktail sticks and strings. Cut into thick slices and arrange on a dish. Pour over the cooking liquid and serve hot with fresh, steamed spinach.

Serves 4–6
Preparation Time: *40–45 minutes*
Cooking Time: *1¼–1½ hours*
Oven temperature: *180°C/350°F/Gas Mark 4*

clipboard: To prepare turkey fillets, place on a board and with a small knife held parallel to the board, make a cut right through the thickest side. Cut almost through to the other edge right down the length of the fillet, then open it out and flatten it well. Remove the white sinew, which is clearly visible, with the point of a knife.

Roast Turkey
with juniper and pomegranates

1 x 2 kg/4 lb oven ready turkey with giblets
50 g/2 oz butter, diced
150 ml/¼ pint olive oil
4 juniper berries
2 rosemary sprigs, (1 to garnish)
200 ml/7 fl oz dry white wine
2 pomegranates
juice of ½ lemon
4 tablespoons Chicken Stock (see page 11)
salt and freshly ground black pepper

sprinkle the turkey inside and out with salt, then place one-third of the butter in the cavity. Sew the opening with trussing thread or string. Place the turkey in an oiled roasting tin.

top with the remaining butter, 7 tablespoons of oil, the juniper berries and rosemary, then pour in the wine. Roast in a preheated moderate oven at 180°C/350°F/Gas Mark 4 for 1½ hours, basting the turkey occasionally with the wine and cooking juices.

add the juice of 1 pomegranate and cook for a further 1 hour or until the turkey is almost tender.

meanwhile, chop the turkey liver and gizzard finely. Heat the remaining oil in a heavy pan, add the liver and gizzard and fry until browned. Remove from the heat and set aside.

add the juice of another pomegranate and salt and pepper to taste to the turkey. Roast for a further 10 minutes, then lift out the turkey and cut into serving pieces. Arrange in an ovenproof serving dish.

skim off the fat from the cooking juices and place the pan over moderate heat. Add the lemon juice and stock and boil until reduced by about half. Strain and stir into the giblet mixture. Pour this sauce over the turkey pieces and return to the oven for a further 7–8 minutes. Serve immediately, garnished with a sprig of fresh rosemary..

Serves 8
Preparation time: *30 minutes*
Cooking time: *2 hours 50 minutes*
Oven temperature: *180°C/350°F/Gas Mark 4*

Braised Pheasant
with savoury risotto

Italians are very fond of wild food and this is one of many excellent recipes for pheasant and other game.

1 x 1.25 kg/2½ lb pheasant, cleaned
salt
4 streaky bacon rashers, derinded
4 tablespoons olive oil
1 onion, chopped
1 carrot, chopped
1 celery stick, chopped
1 bay leaf
150 ml/¼ pint Chicken Stock (see page 11)

Risotto
50 g/2 oz butter
1 small onion, chopped
325 g/11 oz Arborio rice
3–4 tablespoons dry white wine
1 litre/1¾ pints hot Chicken Stock (see page 11)
50 g/2 oz Parmesan cheese, grated
freshly ground black pepper

sprinkle the pheasant inside and out with salt, then wrap the bacon around the outside and secure with string.

heat the oil in a flameproof casserole, add the chopped vegetables and the bay leaf and fry gently until lightly coloured. Add the pheasant and fry until browned on all sides, then lower the heat, cover and cook gently for 40 minutes until the pheasant is tender, adding a little stock from time to time to prevent sticking.

meanwhile, make the risotto. Melt the butter in a heavy pan, add the onion and cook gently for 5 minutes. Add the rice and stir for 2–3 minutes over moderate heat, then add the wine and boil until reduced, stirring constantly. Continue cooking for 20 minutes, adding the stock a cupful at a time, as the liquid is absorbed.

remove from the heat, stir in the Parmesan and salt and pepper to taste, then turn into a warmed serving dish. Remove the pheasant from the casserole and place on top of the risotto. Spoon over the cooking liquid. Serve immediately.

Serves 4–6
Preparation time: *30 minutes*
Cooking time: *1 hour 10 minutes*

Wild Rabbit

braised with red wine and olives

*Wild rabbit has wonderful, herb-scented flesh,
and this recipe brings out its flavour to perfection.*

7 tablespoons olive oil

1 x 1.25 kg/2½ lb wild rabbit, cut into serving pieces

2 garlic cloves, chopped

1 rosemary sprig, chopped

200 ml/ 7 fl oz red wine

6–8 tablespoons Chicken Stock (see page 11)

2 tomatoes, skinned (see page 20) and mashed

250 g/8 oz black olives, halved and pitted

salt and freshly ground black pepper

heat the oil in a flameproof casserole, add the rabbit and sprinkle with the garlic and rosemary.

fry gently until the rabbit is browned on all sides, turning frequently.

add the wine and salt and pepper to taste. Cover and simmer for 30 minutes, adding a little stock to moisten as necessary.

add the tomatoes and olives and cook for a further 40 minutes until the rabbit is tender. Serve hot on a bed of tagliatelle.

Serves 4
Preparation time: *10 minutes*
Cooking time: *1¼ hours*

clipboard: Try and get wild rabbit if possible, as the flavour is so much better than the farmed variety. Many of the larger supermarkets stock it, and it is worth searching out a butcher who sells rabbit and other game. If you are not able to find it, use farmed rabbit — it will still taste very good.

Rabbit Casserole
with fennel and bacon

The smoky flavours of fennel and ham combine beautifully with rabbit. Serve this with pasta and a green salad.

250 g/8 oz fennel (green part only), quartered
3 garlic cloves, peeled
1 x 1.25 kg/2½ lb rabbit, with liver
125 g/4 oz bacon or raw ham
7 tablespoons olive oil
125 g/4 oz fresh breadcrumbs, soaked in a little milk and squeezed dry
salt and freshly ground black pepper
fennel slivers, to garnish

cover the fennel and 2 cloves of garlic in boiling salted water and cook for 15 minutes. Drain thoroughly, reserving the cooking liquid, but discarding the garlic. Chop the fennel finely.

mince the liver together with the bacon or raw ham and the remaining garlic. Heat 2 tablespoons oil in a flameproof casserole, add the fennel and liver mixture.

cook gently for 10 minutes, then mix with the breadcrumbs and salt and pepper to taste. Stuff the rabbit with this mixture, then sew up the opening with trussing thread or string.

place the rabbit in a roasting tin and sprinkle with the remaining oil and salt and pepper to taste.

cover with foil and roast in a preheated oven at 180°C/350°F/Gas Mark 4 for 1½ hours or until the rabbit is tender, basting occasionally with the fennel cooking liquid. Transfer the rabbit to a serving platter garnished with fennel. Serve hot.

Serves 4
Preparation time: *15–20 minutes*
Cooking time: *2 hours*
Oven temperature: *180°C/350°F/Gas Mark 4*

Hare Casserole

Hare is very strongly flavoured, and the aromatic marinade of juniper and peppercorns enhances its taste.

1 medium hare, jointed
1 x quantity marinade (see clipboard below)
50 g/2 oz seasoned flour
50 g/2 oz butter
2 tablespoons olive oil
2 tablespoons brandy
salt and pepper

place the pieces of hare in a deep bowl with the vegetables, herbs, spices, red wine and vinegar of the marinade. Cover and refrigerate for 24–48 hours, turning the hare from time to time in the liquid.

remove the hare from the marinade and drain until dry. Coat the hare with seasoned flour. Heat the butter and oil in a flameproof casserole and brown the hare on all sides.

pour all the marinade into the pan and season to taste with salt. Bring to the boil, cover and cook in a preheated oven at 190°C/375°F/Gas Mark 5 for about 2 hours until the hare is tender.

remove the hare from the casserole and place on a hot serving dish. Remove the herbs and spices from the pan and purée the vegetables in the sauce in a food processor or liquidizer. Return to the casserole and adjust the consistency of the sauce and the seasoning if necessary. Add the brandy, bring to the boil, then pour over the hare and serve hot with pasta.

Serves 4–6
Preparation time: *30–40 minutes, plus marinating*
Cooking time: *2¼–2¾ hours*
Oven temperature: *190°C/375°F/Gas Mark 5*

clipboard: Marinades tenderize game and meat and gives extra flavour. This is a typical recipe: 1 carrot, celery stick and large onion, all neatly sliced, 1–2 garlic cloves, crushed, 6–8 parsley stalks, 1 sprig thyme or rosemary, 2 bay leaves, 4 juniper berries, 8 peppercorns, 600 ml/1 pint red wine.

Venison *with brandy and redcurrant sauce*

625–750 g/1¼–1½ lb venison, diced
1 quantity marinade (see page 164)
2 tablespoons olive oil
125 g/4 oz rindless streaky bacon, diced
2–3 tablespoons seasoned flour
6–8 tablespoons redcurrant jelly
2 tablespoons grappa or brandy
salt and pepper

place the venison and marinade in a bowl, cover and refrigerate for at least 24 hours, turning the venison from time to time. Remove the meat from the marinade and drain until dry.

heat the oil in a pan and cook the bacon until golden brown. Remove from the pan. Toss the venison in the seasoned flour and brown it on all sides in the hot oil.

add the bacon and the marinade. Season lightly, cover and simmer gently on top of the stove, or cook in a preheated oven at 180°C/350°F/Gas Mark 4 for 1½–2 hours.

remove the venison from the pan, cover and keep hot. Strain the cooking liquid into a clean pan and whisk in 2 tablespoons of redcurrant jelly. Boil until the sauce reduces to a thin coating consistency. Pour over the meat and keep hot.

melt the remaining redcurrant jelly in a pan and whisk until smooth. Add the grappa or brandy and boil for about one minute. Pour into a sauce boat and serve separately.

Serves 4–6
Preparation time: *30–35 minutes, plus 24 hours marinating*
Cooking time: *1½–2½ hours*
Oven temperature: *180°C/350°F/Gas Mark 4*

clipboard: For this dish, casserole or shoulder venison is ideal. It is quite reasonable to buy, the price being comparable with other braising meats. Venison is a very lean meat.

Pizza, Rice
and Polenta

Basic Dough
for home-made pizza

It is so useful to be able to make your own pizza from scratch, and this recipe gives excellent results.

25 g/1 oz fresh yeast
300 ml/½ pint tepid water
425 g/14 oz strong plain flour, plus extra for working the dough
1 teaspoon salt

blend the yeast with a little of the tepid water. Sieve the flour and salt into a large mixing bowl.

make a well in the centre and pour in the yeast mixture and the remaining tepid water. Using your hand and with a circular movement, gradually work the flour into the liquid moving from the centre of the well outwards to form a sticky, elastic dough.

turn out the dough on to a floured working surface and knead it well, adding more flour if necessary, until it stops sticking to your knuckles and the working surface. Knead for approximately 10 minutes until it is smooth and elastic. At this stage, if you are making more than one pizza, divide the dough into the required number of pieces and knead each one into a ball.

sprinkle the bottom of the mixing bowl with flour and leave the dough to rise, covering the bowl with a cloth for approximately 1 hour. The time required will depend on the warmth of the kitchen. The dough is ready for rolling out when it has doubled in size.

Serves 4: makes 2 large, 4 small pizzas
Preparation time: *10 minutes, plus kneading and rising*

clipboard: This amount of dough can be shaped into two large round pizzas, approximately 30 cm/12 inches in diameter, one large rectangular pizza, or four individual pizzas approximately 20 cm/8 inches in diameter. Pizza tins will help you shape the pizza better than simple baking trays. The dough is spread thin, about 5 mm/¼ inch.

Fresh Pizza

with onions and eggs

Pizzas are said to have been invented by frugal Neapolitans as a way to use up bread dough. This recipe shows how you can achieve delicious, authentic results from the simplest of ingredients.

4–5 tablespoons olive oil
750 g–1 kg/1½–2 lb onions, finely sliced
½ quantity basic pizza dough (see page 170)
2–3 hard-boiled eggs, sliced
salt and pepper
1–2 tablespoons chopped parsley, to garnish

heat 3–4 tablespoons oil in a pan and cook the onions over moderate heat until they are soft and lightly coloured. Season well with salt and pepper.

roll out the dough to 2 x 30 cm/12 inch circles and place on a baking tray. Spread the cooked onions over the surface.

bake in a preheated oven at 230°C/450°F/Gas Mark 8 for 15–20 minutes until the pizzas are risen and golden brown.

arrange the slices of hard-boiled egg over the top, sprinkle with the remainder of the oil and return to the oven for a further 2–3 minutes. Sprinkle chopped parsley over just before serving.

Serves 2
Preparation time: *20 minutes*
Cooking time: *15–20 minutes*
Oven temperature:*230°C/450°F/Gas Mark 8*

clipboard: This pizza recipe can be served hot or cold. If it is to be served cold, do not return it to the oven after the hard-boiled eggs have been arranged on top.

Easter Pizza

Easter is a joyous time in Italy, and many traditional dishes are served then, including this festive pizza

3 eggs

75 g/3 oz Parmesan cheese, grated

75 g/3 oz pecorino cheese, grated

1 quantity basic pizza dough, unrisen (see page 170)

125 ml/4 fl oz olive oil

150 g/5 oz strong white flour

175–250 g/6–8 oz salami

1–2 hard-boiled eggs, sliced

a little extra olive oil

salt and freshly ground black pepper

black olive, to garnish

beat the eggs and cheeses together, and season with salt. Knead the pizza dough well and press out into a small circle. Pour some of the olive oil and flour into the centre. Fold over the edges, press out into a circle again and repeat the process until all the oil and flour have been incorporated. Knead until smooth.

press out into a larger circle and place the egg mixture in the centre. Fold over and knead well until it is incorporated into the dough. Place in an oiled bowl, cover and keep in a warm place for 1–1½ hours until doubled in size.

turn out on to a board, knead into a circle and place in a greased 25 cm/10 inch cake tin. Cover and leave to prove until doubled in size. Bake in a preheated oven at 230°C/450°F/Gas Mark 8 for 20–30 minutes until it sounds hollow when tapped.

turn out on to a baking tray and return to the oven, upside down, for a few minutes until golden brown. Arrange the salami, hard-boiled eggs and olive on top. Sprinkle olive oil over the eggs and return to the oven for a few minutes to warm through. Serve immediately, sprinkled with black pepper.

Serves 8–10
Preparation time: *30 minutes, plus rising and proving*
Cooking time: *25–30 minutes*
Oven temperature: *230°C/450°F/Gas Mark 8*

clipboard: If this pizza is too large for your requirements, you can make half the quantity and bake it in an 18–20 cm/7–8 inch tin. However, you must use the same amount of yeast in the pizza dough as is given for the full quantity.

Saffron Risotto
with sausage and peppers

Fragrant and colourful, this is a luscious risotto.
It should be made with Arborio rice for the best results.

pinch of saffron stamens
3 tablespoons olive oil
I small carrot, finely chopped
I red onion, finely chopped
I stick celery, finely chopped
250 g/8 oz Italian sausage, diced
2 fresh sage leaves
2 red and green peppers, cored, deseeded
and cut into strips
I x 400 g/14 oz can whole tomatoes, drained,
deseeded and chopped
375 g/12 oz Arborio rice
50–75 g/2–3 oz Parmesan cheese, grated
salt and freshly ground black pepper
sprig fresh sage leaves, to garnish

place the saffron in a small bowl, pour on 2 tablespoons boiling water and leave until required.

heat the oil and brown the carrot, onion, celery and sausage. Add the sage and peppers and cook for a few minutes, then add the tomatoes and half the juice from the can. Season and continue to cook for about 30 minutes, adding more juice if necessary, until the vegetables are tender and most of the juice has evaporated.

meanwhile, cook the rice in a large pan of boiling salted water for 12–15 minutes until just tender, then drain well, return to the pan and stir in the saffron. Mix in well so that all the rice is yellow. If necessary, stir over a gentle heat until the rice is dry.

stir in the vegetable and sausage mix and Parmesan to taste. Pile into an ovenproof dish and cook in a preheated oven at 200°C/400°F/Gas Mark 6 for 5–10/10–15 minutes until golden brown. Serve hot, garnished with sage.

Serves 4
Preparation time: *20–25 minutes*
Cooking time: *50–60 minutes*
Oven temperature: *200°C/400°F/Gas Mark 6*

clipboard: You can buy powdered saffron or whole stamens, both of which are used in the same way. If you are unable to obtain saffron, use a little turmeric to colour the rice.

Creamy Risotto
with Fontina and Gorgonzola cheese

375 g/12 oz long-grain rice
150 g/5 oz Fontina cheese
150 g/5 oz Gorgonzola cheese
450 ml/¾ pint milk
75 g/3 oz butter
40 g/1½ oz plain flour
175 ml/6 fl oz single cream
salt and pepper

boil the rice in salted water, and drain when just tender.

remove the rind from the Fontina, cut into cubes and place in a bowl. Cut the Gorgonzola into very small pieces. Put the milk in a small pan over a low heat.

soften two-thirds of the butter in a pan, add the flour, stirring well, then gradually add the hot milk, stirring continuously to make a sauce.

add the small pieces of Gorgonzola gradually, season with a pinch of salt and pepper. Remove from the heat and stir in the cream.

add the drained rice to the bowl with the cubed Fontina and mix with the remaining butter.

make a layer of rice in a buttered ovenproof dish, cover with one-third of the Gorgonzola sauce, add another layer of rice followed by half the remaining Gorgonzola sauce, and repeat for the third time.

place the dish in a moderate oven at 180°C/350°F/Gas Mark 4 for 10 minutes, then serve immediately. For the best results, the rice needs to be very hot but the sauce on the top should not be brown.

Serves 4
Preparation time: *10 minutes*
Cooking time: *30–40 minutes*
Oven temperature: *180°C/350°F/Gas Mark 4*

Polenta

with Fontina cheese

Polenta is one of the basic staples of Italian cooking — as basic as mashed potatoes! It is made from maize flour, which gives it its distinctive, golden colour.

2 litres/3½ pints water
325 g/11 oz fine polenta
250 g/8 oz Fontina cheese, diced
50 g/2 oz Parmesan cheese, grated
150 g/5 oz butter, melted
salt and freshly ground black pepper

bring the water to the boil in a large pan, add the polenta gradually in a thin, steady stream, stirring all the time.

add salt and pepper to taste and stir well to mix.

add the Fontina and cook very gently for 8 minutes (or 45 minutes if you are not using quick-cook polenta), stirring frequently.

pour the polenta into a shallow dish and sprinkle with the Parmesan and a little pepper. Pour the melted butter over the top and serve immediately.

Serves 4–6
Preparation time: *10 minutes*
Cooking time: *45 minutes*

Clipboard: Polenta has to be stirred continuously during cooking to avoid lumps. Buy the instant or quick-cooking type of polenta from an Italian delicatessen or large supermarket, otherwise you will find it hard work. Polenta spits and splutters during cooking, so take care while standing over the pan, and use a long-handled spoon.

Country Risotto
with mixed vegetables

A healthy, fresh-tasting risotto is always welcome. What's more, this recipe can be varied according to what vegetables you have available.

50 g/2 oz butter
2 tablespoons olive oil
1 large onion, finely chopped
2 garlic cloves, crushed
125 g/4 oz fresh shelled or frozen peas
125 g/4 oz small fresh asparagus tips
175–250 g/6–8 oz small courgettes, sliced
425 g/14 oz Arborio rice
500 g/1 lb tomatoes, skinned (see page 20), deseeded and chopped or 1 x 425 g/14 oz can whole tomatoes, drained, deseeded and chopped
1.25 litres/2¼ pints Chicken Stock (see page 11)
2–3 tablespoons grated Parmesan cheese
salt and pepper
fresh basil leaves, to garnish

heat the butter and oil in a heavy-based pan and cook the onion and garlic until soft and lightly coloured.

add the fresh peas now if using, also the asparagus and courgettes and cook for 2–3 minutes. Stir in the rice and mix well. Add the tomatoes and the stock a little at a time. Season to taste with salt and pepper.

mix well and cook gently for about 18 minutes, adding more hot stock or water if necessary to keep the rice moist. If you are using frozen peas add them 5 minutes before the end of the cooking time. When the rice is tender, check the seasoning and stir in the Parmesan to taste.

transfer to a serving dish and sprinkle with the basil just before serving. Serve hot.

Serves 4
Preparation time: *25–30 minutes*
Cooking time: *35–40 minutes*

Clipboard: Any selection of vegetables can be used in this recipe, including French beans, broad beans, sliced mushrooms or peppers.

Risotto
with wild mushrooms

125 g/4 oz butter
1 onion, finely chopped
375 g/12 oz wild mushrooms (see clipboard below)
or oyster mushrooms, thinly sliced
500 g/1 lb Arborio rice
1.2 litres/2 pints boiling Chicken Stock (see page 11)
⅛ teaspoon powdered saffron or saffron threads
40 g/1½ oz grated Parmesan cheese, plus a little
extra to serve
salt and freshly ground black pepper

heat half of the butter in a large, heavy-based frying pan, add the onion and fry gently until it is soft and translucent. Take care that it does not become too coloured.

add the sliced mushrooms and cook for 2–3 minutes, stirring occasionally. Add the rice and stir over a moderately low heat until all the grains are glistening and beginning to turn translucent around the edges.

stir in a ladleful of boiling stock and simmer very gently until it has been absorbed. Continue adding more stock in this manner until the rice is thoroughly cooked and tender and all the liquid has been absorbed. This will take about 15–20 minutes.

stir in the saffron halfway through cooking. Stir frequently to prevent the rice sticking to the base of the pan, and season with salt and pepper.

when the rice is ready, gently mix in the remaining butter and the Parmesan. The risotto should not be too dry, in fact, it should be quite moist. Serve with extra grated Parmesan.

Serves 4
Preparation time: *5 minutes*
Cooking time: *30 minutes*

Clipboard: Any fresh wild mushroom will taste good in risotto, but dried wild mushrooms are available in packets from supermarkets; Italian delicatessens also sell them loose. They may seem expensive, but they are only used in very small quantities. Before use, put them in a bowl, cover with warm water and leave them to soak for 20–30 minutes.

Seafood Risotto
with mussels and scallops

One of the pleasures of risotto is that you can vary the ingredients — so use whatever fresh shellfish is available at your fishmonger.

600 ml/1 pint fresh mussels in their shells
4 tablespoons olive oil
1 onion, chopped
2 garlic cloves, crushed
375g/12 oz Arborio rice
1.8 litres/3 pints Fish Stock (see page 11)
125 ml/4 fl oz dry white wine
few strands of saffron
350 g/12 oz peeled cooked prawns
250 g/8 oz prepared scallops
250 g/8 oz prepared squid
salt and freshly ground black pepper

To garnish
2 tablespoons chopped fresh parsley
sprigs of fresh oregano

prepare the mussels: cover with cold water and discard any that are cracked or open, or rise to the surface. Scrub well to remove any barnacles, remove the beards and soak in fresh cold water until ready to cook. Place in a large saucepan with a little water and oil, covered, until they open. Shake the pan occasionally. Drain and set aside, reserving the cooking liquid.

heat the olive oil in a large deep frying pan, add the onion and garlic and fry gently until they are soft and golden, stirring occasionally.

stir in the rice and cook over low heat for 1–2 minutes, stirring until the grains are glistening with oil and almost translucent. Pour in some of the fish stock and the reserved mussel liquid and wine, and bring to the boil.

meanwhile, soak the saffron in a little boiling water and add to the risotto with the prepared prawns, scallops and squid. Reduce the heat to a simmer and cook gently, adding more fish stock as necessary until the rice is tender and creamy and all the liquid has been absorbed. Garnish with chopped parsley and sprigs of oregano.

Serves 4–6
Preparation time: *25 minutes*
Cooking time: *45 minutes*

Chicken Risotto
with white wine and tomatoes

1 x 1 kg/2lb oven ready chicken
2 litres/3½ pints water
2 celery sticks
2 onions
2 carrots
3–4 tablespoons olive oil
7 tablespoons white wine
375 g/12 oz tomatoes, skinned (see page 20) and mashed
500 g/1 lb Arborio rice
75 g/3 oz butter, softened
75 g/3 oz Parmesan cheese, grated
salt and freshly ground black pepper

remove the bones from the chicken and place them in a large pan with the water. Add 1 celery stick, 1 onion and 1 carrot, and season liberally with salt and pepper.

bring to the boil, lower the heat, cover and simmer for 1½ hours. Strain the stock and keep hot.

meanwhile dice the chicken meat, removing all the skin. Finely chop the remaining vegetables and fry gently in the olive oil until lightly coloured.

add the chicken and fry for a further 5 minutes, stirring constantly, then add the wine and boil until it evaporates.

add the tomatoes and salt and pepper to taste. Cover and cook gently for 20 minutes, adding a little of the chicken stock if the mixture becomes dry.

stir in the rice, then add 200 ml/7 fl oz chicken stock. Cook for 20–25 minutes until the rice is just tender, adding a little more stock to moisten, as necessary.

remove from the heat, add the butter and Parmesan and fold in gently to mix. Serve immediately sprinkled with freshly ground black pepper..

Serves 6
Preparation time: *35 minutes*
Cooking time: *1–2 hours*

Risotto alla Milanese

Melting, creamy and utterly luxurious, this risotto is justifiably famous all over the world. The finest quality rice is grown south of Milan, and the region is renowned for its superb rice dishes.

150 g/5 oz butter
½ onion, chopped
7 tablespoons dry white wine
1 litre/1¾ pints hot Beef Stock (see page 10)
425 g/14 oz Arborio rice
¼ teaspoon saffron powder
125 g/4 oz Parmesan cheese, grated
4 tablespoons cream
salt and freshly ground black pepper

melt half the butter in a large, heavy-based pan, add the onion and a little pepper and fry gently until golden. Add the wine and 7 tablespoons of the stock. Boil until reduced by half.

add the rice and cook for 5 minutes, stirring constantly, then add the saffron and salt and pepper to taste.

continue cooking for 20 minutes, stirring in the hot stock a cup at a time as the liquid is absorbed, until the rice is just tender.

remove from the heat, stir in the remaining butter, the Parmesan and cream and leave to stand for 1 minute. Sprinkle with freshly ground black pepper and serve.

Serves 4–6
Preparation time: *10 minutes*
Cooking time: *35 minutes*

Vegetables and Salads

Mixed Vegetable Salad

A mixture of cooked vegetables makes quite a substantial meal and, as in many Italian dishes, the ingredients may vary according to the vegetables that are available.

3–4 firm tomatoes, sliced
375–500 g/12 oz–1 lb small new potatoes, scraped, cooked and sliced
125 g/4 oz cooked or canned chickpeas
250 g/8 oz cooked French beans, trimmed, cut in half and cooked
125 g/4 oz cooked or canned red beans
4–5 spring onions, sliced
1 tablespoon chopped fresh basil
50–75 ml/2–3 fl oz olive oil
2 tablespoons red or white wine vinegar
salt and freshly ground black pepper
fresh basil, to garnish

arrange the sliced tomatoes around the edge of a shallow salad bowl or a deep plate. Pile the potatoes into one quarter of the dish.

pile the chick peas next to them, then the French beans and finally the red beans. If you are using canned chickpeas and red beans, drain them well before adding to the salad.

sprinkle the spring onions around the edge of the dish and the chopped basil over the vegetables, and refrigerate until required.

whisk together the oil and vinegar, and season well with salt and pepper. Just before serving, whisk the oil and vinegar again and pour over the salad.

Serves 4–6
Preparation time: *25–30 minutes*

clipboard: If you wish, a crushed clove of garlic can be added to the oil and vinegar. When cooking the French beans, leave them slightly crisp so they give 'bite' to the salad. Remember that dried beans and chickpeas need to be soaked thoroughly before cooking.

Tomato Salad
with anchovies and cumin

The combined flavours of tomato, mustard, anchovies and cumin make a biting, piquant salad. For a more substantial dish, this is often garnished with slices of hard-boiled egg.

1 heaped tablespoon French mustard

2 tablespoons white or red wine vinegar

75 ml/3 fl oz olive oil

4–5 firm tomatoes, sliced

1 stick celery, cut into thin finger-length strips

1 red onion, diced

1 teaspoon cumin seeds

2 anchovy fillets, chopped

salt and pepper

2 hard-boiled eggs to garnish, (optional)

place the mustard in a small bowl and stir in the vinegar. Season lightly with salt and plenty of pepper.

whisk in the olive oil until the mixture is well blended.

place the tomatoes in a salad bowl with the celery, onion, cumin seeds and anchovy fillets.

pour on the dressing, mix well, garnish with the hard-boiled eggs if using, and serve.

Serves 4
Preparation time: *20 minutes*

clipboard: Italian red onions are ideal for this salad. They look attractive and have a sweet taste. If they are not available, chopped spring onions make a good alternative.

Braised Zucchini
with mozzarella and tomatoes

*Courgettes have a great affinity with tomato sauce,
and this is a way of giving them a robust,
hearty flavour.*

2 tablespoons oil
25 g/1 oz butter
1 shallot, chopped
6 courgettes, cut into 5 cm/2 inch sticks
1 x 375g/12 oz can plum tomatoes
2 tablespoons Chicken Stock (see page 11)
20 black olives, halved and pitted
¼ teaspoon chopped oregano
1 tablespoon chopped parsley
1 Mozzarella cheese, cubed
salt and pepper

heat the oil and butter in a large, shallow pan, add the chopped shallot and cook over a low heat until softened.

add the courgettes and cook for a few minutes over a high heat, then reduce it to medium.

add the tomatoes, mashed with a fork, season with salt and pepper and cook until the courgettes are tender, adding a little stock if necessary.

add the halved and pitted olives, oregano and parsley. Cube the Mozzarella cheese and scatter over the top. Cover the pan, switch off the heat and leave to stand for a few minutes before serving.

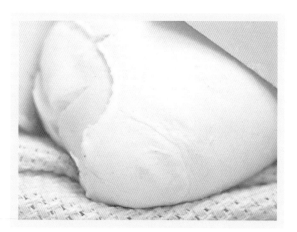

Serves 4
Preparation time: *20 minutes*
Cooking time: *20 minutes*

Cheeses

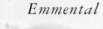

Dolcelatte

Emmental

Parmesan

Gorgonzola

Gorgonzola

Gorgonzola is a creamy yellow semi-soft cheese with distinctive blue-green veins and a rich, strong flavour. It was first produced over a thousand years ago in Gorgonzola, a village in the north of Italy, and is one of the world's oldest cheeses. It can be used in cooking or eaten by itself and is often served with fresh fruit such as apples and pears.

Emmental

Emmental is a world-famous hard cheese which is pale yellow in colour and made from cows' milk. It has a delicately mild, nutty flavour. Originating from Switzerland it is easily recognised by the large, evenly spaced holes which are distributed throughout the cheese. Emmental is equally good as a dessert and when used for cooking.

Parmesan

Parmesan is Parma's famous, cow's milk cheese, which is hard and grainy textured. It is pale yellow in colour with a strong flavour and aroma. It can be left to mature for up to 3 years. It is sold in a block and is generally grated finely and sprinkled over dishes. It can also be bought grated in a vacuum pack but it is always best to buy it in a block if possible.

Dolcelatte

Dolcelatte is a factory-made cheese, a mass produced version of Gorgonzola. It has the same, characteristic blue veins. Although it doesn't claim the classic status of that great cheese, it is nevertheless very agreeable in its own right. It has a creamy velvet-smooth texture and a mild, sweet taste. The translation of dolcelatte is 'sweet milk'.

Bel Paese

Fontina

Pecorino Romano

Mozzarella

Bel Paese

Bel Paese is a relatively modern invention, and is one of the world's most popular 'easy-eating' cheeses. It is a soft cheese which has a creamy, mild flavour, and a shiny yellow rind. It is made from cow's milk. Bel Paese was first made in the 1920's in Lombardy in Italy, but it is now produced all over Europe. The name means 'beautiful country'.

Mozzarella

Mozzarella is a white curd cheese with a soft, chewy texture and a mild, milky flavour. It is moulded into balls and wrapped in small bags with whey added to keep it moist. Originally it was only made from buffalo's milk, but it is now more oftenmade from cow's milk, or a mixture of both. It is eaten fresh, or used in cooking, for pizza or pasta.

Pecorino Romano

Pecorino Romano is a hard, grating cheese not dissimilar to Parmesan. It has been made for two thousand years in Southern Italy. The main ingredient is sheep's milk, and this gives the cheese a very distinctive salty, tangy taste. The name is taken from the word 'pecora' which means ewe. There are several kinds of pecorino, which is used like Parmesan.

Fontina

Genuine Fontina is made exclusively in the Val d'Aosta region of northern Italy. Fontina is reminiscent of Swiss Gruyère, but it is softer and sweeter with much smaller holes. It is a really superb table cheese — soft but sliceable and pale yellow in colour. Fontina is made from cow's milk, and is good for cooking, as well as for eating by itself.

Fresh Asparagus
with tarragon sauce

1.5 kg/3 lb asparagus
40 g/1½ oz tuna in oil
2 anchovy fillets
200 ml/7 fl oz olive oil
2 tablespoons white wine
2 tablespoons chopped tarragon
2 hard-boiled eggs
juice of ¼ lemon
salt and white pepper
few sprigs of fresh tarragon, to garnish

trim off the woody ends from the asparagus and scrape the tough skin at the lower ends. Rinse under cold running water. Divide into bundles and tie up with string. Stand in a tall pan containing enough boiling salted water to come two-thirds of the way up, and cover the tips with a kitchen foil dome. Simmer for 8–18 minutes, depending on the thickness of the asparagus.

meanwhile, prepare the sauce: drain and chop the tuna and anchovies. Put in a blender or food processor with 2–3 tablespoons of the oil, the wine and the tarragon.

sieve the hard-boiled egg yolks into a bowl and beat to a paste with a wooden spoon. Add a pinch of salt, then slowly trickle in a few drops of oil. Stir in one direction and add more oil once the first few drops have been absorbed. Continue until all the oil has been used up and the mixture is thick and smooth.

add the mixture to the blender with the lemon juice, season with a pinch of salt if necessary and a little pepper. Blend briefly to mix the ingredients.

drain the asparagus and cut off the white ends (reserve for soup or stock). Arrange on a heated serving plate and pour over the sauce. Sieve the hard-boiled egg whites over the asparagus before serving, and garnish with a few sprigs of fresh tarragon.

Serves 4
Preparation time: *15 minutes*
Cooking time: *8–18 minutes*

Peas and Onions
with ham

This is a quick variant on the classic 'piselli alla Romana', fresh peas with ham. If you have prosciutto available, the dish will taste even better.

8–12 pickling onions
50 g/2 oz butter
500 g/1 lb fresh shelled or frozen peas
300 ml/½ pint Chicken Stock (see page 12)
50 g/2 oz ham, cut into strips
salt and pepper

blanch the onions in boiling salted water for 4–5 minutes. Drain well. Melt the butter in a pan, add the onions and cook gently until golden.

add the fresh peas if using and 150 ml/¼ pint stock. Season with salt and pepper. Continue cooking gently for 15–20 minutes until the peas and onions are tender.

add more stock if it is necessary, but you should allow most of it to boil away by the time the peas are cooked.

if frozen peas are used, add the stock to the onions, and cook until they are nearly tender, then add the peas and cook for 4–5 minutes.

stir in the ham just before the peas are cooked. Check the seasoning and pour into a serving dish.

Serves 4–6
Preparation time: *10–20 minutes*
Cooking time: *30–35 minutes*

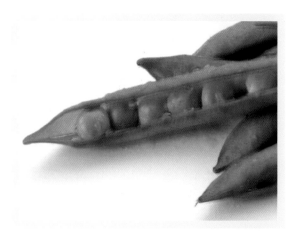

Peperonata

Peppers, tomatoes, onions and garlic braised in olive oil are the simple ingredients of this colourful Italian classic. It is equally delicious served hot or cold.

100 ml/3½ fl oz olive oil
375 g/12 oz onions, finely sliced
2 garlic cloves, crushed
500 g/1 lb red and yellow peppers, cored, deseeded and quartered
500 g/1 lb ripe tomatoes, peeled and chopped or 1 x 425 g/14 oz can chopped tomatoes
salt and freshly ground black pepper

heat the oil in a heavy-based pan and gently fry the onions and garlic until they are lightly coloured.

add the peppers, cover and cook over a gentle heat for 10–12 minutes.

add the tomatoes and season well with salt and pepper.

cook uncovered, until the peppers are tender and the liquid has reduced to a thick sauce. Check the seasoning and pour into a serving dish. The peperonata can be served hot or cold.

Serves 4
Preparation Time: *20 minutes*
Cooking Time: *40–45 minutes*

clipboard: If canned tomatoes are used, raise the heat toward the end of the cooking time to evaporate the extra liquid. If you prefer, the peppers can be skinned before being cooked.

Stuffed Zucchini
with ricotta and Parmesan

Courgettes are excellent when baked with a savoury stuffing, and this recipe is particularly good.

6 courgettes
25 g/1 oz crustless white bread
milk for soaking
125 g/4 oz ricotta or soft curd cheese
¼ teaspoon dried oregano
1 garlic clove, crushed
40 g/1½ oz Parmesan cheese, grated
1 egg yolk
salt and freshly ground black pepper

trim the ends from the courgettes and cook in a large saucepan of boiling salted water for 5 minutes. Drain well. Soak the bread in a little milk until soft and then squeeze dry.

cut the courgettes in half lengthways and carefully scoop out the centres using a teaspoon. You should be left with long boat-shaped cases which are ready for filling.

chop the courgette centres finely and place in a bowl. Add the bread, ricotta or soft curd cheese, oregano, garlic, Parmesan, egg yolk, salt and freshly ground black pepper. Mix thoroughly. The consistency should be fairly soft. If it is too stiff, add a little milk.

arrange the courgette cases close together in a single layer in a well-oiled shallow baking tray or ovenproof dish. Fill the cases with the cheese mixture and bake in a preheated oven at 190°C/375°F/Gas Mark 5 for 35–40 minutes until the courgettes are tender and the filling is golden brown. Serve immediately.

Serves 4
Preparation time: *20 minutes*
Cooking time: *40–45 minutes*
Oven temperature: *190°C/375°F/Gas Mark 5*

Cannellini Beans
with bacon and sage

This is a farmer-style recipe from the Italian countryside. Cannellini beans not only have a lovely flavour themselves, but also enhance that of the other ingredients.

500 g/1 lb dried cannellini beans, soaked overnight
1 celery stalk, chopped
2 bay leaves
125 g/4 oz bacon, derinded
50 g/2 oz bacon fat
3 tablespoons oil
½ onion, chopped
1 tablespoon chopped sage leaves
sprig of rosemary
garlic clove
3 ripe plum tomatoes, skinned (see page 20), chopped and deseeded or 1 x 200g/7oz can tomatoes,
drained, deseeded and chopped
½ chicken stock cube
2 tablespoons red wine
salt and freshly ground black pepper

put the beans in a large pan with 2 litres/3½ pints of water, the chopped celery and the bay leaves. Bring to the boil and simmer for at least 2 hours until tender.

put the bacon in a small pan with enough water to cover and boil for 10 minutes. When cooked, remove the bacon with a slotted spoon and cut into bite-sized pieces.

chop the bacon fat and put in a shallow pan with the oil. Add the chopped onions, herbs and crushed garlic, and cook over a medium heat until the onion is golden.

add the drained cooked beans, mix together, season with salt and plenty of pepper and leave for 10 minutes to allow the flavours to mingle.

add the fresh or canned tomatoes to the pan. Then add the boiled bacon, crumble in the stock cube and stir in the wine. Leave the sauce to thicken a little, then adjust the seasoning and serve hot.

Serves 4
Preparation time: *30 minutes, plus 8 hours soaking*
Cooking time: *3 hours*

Baked Aubergines

with anchovy and pecorino cheese stuffing

625 g/1¼ lb small round aubergines
125 ml/4 fl oz oil
1 onion, finely chopped
4 anchovy fillets, finely chopped
600 g/1¼ lb plum tomatoes, skinned (see page 20), deseeded and chopped
1 heaped tablespoon capers, finely chopped
6 basil leaves, torn, plus a few extra to garnish
50 g/2 oz pecorino cheese, grated
salt and pepper
basil, to garnish

wash and dry the aubergines, then cut off the tops. Slit the flesh from the top into wedge shapes, making cuts just over half-way down the sides with a sharp knife.

sprinkle with salt and leave upside down on an inclined chopping board for 30 minutes to drain off the bitter juices. Rinse well.

heat one-third of the oil in a shallow pan, add the onion and cook over a medium heat until golden. Add the drained anchovies and cook until they are softened.

stir in the tomatoes, capers and basil, and season with pepper. Continue cooking this mixture until the sauce has thickened. Remove from the heat and add the pecorino.

dry the aubergines on absorbent kitchen paper and put them in a baking dish. Open them out a little, fill with the prepared sauce, trickle the remaining oil over the top, and put in a moderate oven at 180°C/350°F/Gas Mark 4 for 30 minutes. Serve immediately, garnished with fresh herbs.

Serves: 4
Preparation time: *15 minutes plus draining*
Cooking time: *45 minutes*
Oven temperature: *180°C/350°F/Gas Mark 4*

Fresh herbs

Rosemary   *Basil*

Fennel

Marjoram

Rosemary
Italians adore Rosemary, and use it extensively. It is a perennial herb with long, spiky green leaves and pale blue flowers. When fresh it is very strongly flavoured and aromatic. It is often used to flavour vinegars and salads. Italians like using it to flavour lamb and sucking pig. It can be bought fresh or dried and is also very easy to cultivate at home

Basil
Basil is arguably the most important herb used in Italian cooking. Its bright green leaves have a unique flavour, and wonderfully spicy aroma. Basil combines beautifully with tomatoes, which are also essential in Italian cooking. It is the main ingredient in *pesto* a very popular basil sauce often served with pasta. Basil is also frequently used in salads.

Fennel
Florence fennel is used extensively in Italian cooking. The bulb and the stalks can be eaten either raw or braised. Fennel is often served as a hot vegetable or eaten raw in salads. The bright green, feathery leaves of wild fennel resemble dill, and are chopped up and used to flavour sauces. The seeds are also used in spiced meats.

Marjoram
Marjoram comes from the same family as oregano. It is a herb with small, grey-green leaves and mauve and white flowers. Marjoram is very aromatic, with a sweet, spicy flavour. It is often associated with chicken, pasta dishes, tomatoes, and other vegetable dishes. It should be added at the end of cooking. In Italy it is used as a variant of oregano or combined with it.

Sage

Juniper

Thyme

Bay leaves

Sage
Sage is a grey-green herb with pink and mauve flowers, and leaves that have a velvety sheen. It is very aromatic with a slightly bitter taste. It features in Italian veal and calf's liver recipes, also in cheese, and pasta dishes. It is widely available fresh or dried.

Juniper
The berries of the juniper bush are dark, and very similar to peppercorns. Juniper is very aromatic, with a spicy perfume. It is especially good with meat, but should be used sparingly as it can be bitter. Juniper is used in pork and game dishes, and in marinades.

Thyme
Thyme is a small, bushy shrub with grcy-green leaves and small pink, mauve, red or white flowers. Thyme has a fragrant aroma and a clove-like taste. Though it is not all that frequently used in Italian cooking it is sometimes used in tomato sauces or marinades, and in *bouquet garni*. It can be bought fresh or dried.

Bay leaves
The leaves of the bay tree are dark green, glossy and pungent. Because of its strong aroma it is used as a herb. Fully grown bay trees are rare, they are mostly grown as a bushy shrub or small tree in a pot or tub. The leaves are used to flavour soups, casseroles, and pasta dishes. Bay leaves are also a vital component of *bouquet garni*.

Vegetable Fritatta

Italian omelettes are similar in style to the Spanish, with all kinds of ingredients incorporated into the basic mixture. You can happily adapt this to any other vegetable that you have available.

3 tablespoons olive oil

2 onions, very finely sliced

3 courgettes, finely sliced

3 tomatoes, skinned (see page 20) and chopped

6 large eggs

50 g/2 oz Parmesan cheese, grated

few fresh basil leaves, torn

1 tablespoon chopped fresh parsley

25 g/1 oz butter

salt and freshly ground black pepper

heat the olive oil in a large, heavy-based frying pan. Add the sliced onions and sauté very gently for 8–10 minutes until really soft, golden brown and almost caramelized. Add the courgettes and continue cooking until golden on both sides, stirring from time to time. Add the tomatoes and cook over moderate heat until the mixture is thick.

break the eggs into a large bowl and add the seasoning, grated Parmesan, torn basil and parsley. Beat well with a wire whisk until all the ingredients are thoroughly blended.

drain off and discard any excess oil from the cooked tomato mixture. Add the mixture to the beaten eggs and stir together gently until they are well mixed.

heat the butter in a large clean frying pan until it is hot and sizzling. Pour in the egg mixture and reduce the heat to a bare simmer (as low as it will go). Cook very gently until the omelette is firm and set underneath. Place under a preheated hot grill for a few seconds to set and brown the top. Slide out on to a plate and serve at room temperature cut into wedges.

Serves 4
Preparation time: *25 minutes*
Cooking time: *10–15 minutes*

Baked Aubergines
with cheese and basil

1.5 kg/3 lb aubergines
125 ml/4 fl oz olive oil
1 onion, finely chopped
2 kg/4 lb tomatoes, skinned (see page 20)
and chopped
3 fresh basil leaves, torn, or 2 teaspoons dried basil
flour for dusting
150 g/5 oz grated Parmesan cheese
250 g/8 oz Mozzarella cheese, finely sliced
salt and freshly ground black pepper

trim the stems from the aubergines and slice them into rounds. Sprinkle each slice with a little salt and place the salted slices in a colander. Cover the aubergines with a plate and add weights to squeeze out the juices. Leave the aubergines to drain for about 30 minutes.

meanwhile make the tomato sauce. Heat 4 tablespoons of the olive oil in a heavy-based frying pan and fry the onion until soft and golden. Add the chopped tomatoes and basil, mix well and simmer gently, uncovered, until the mixture reduces to a thick sauce. Season to taste with salt and pepper.

rinse the aubergine slices thoroughly in cold water to remove the saltiness. Pat dry with absorbent kitchen paper and dust them with flour. Heat a little of the remaining olive oil in a large frying pan and fry the aubergine in batches, adding more oil as needed, until they are cooked and golden brown on both sides. Drain on absorbent kitchen paper.

oil an ovenproof dish and arrange a layer of aubergine slices in the bottom of the dish. Sprinkle with Parmesan and cover with Mozzarella slices. Spoon some of the tomato sauce over the top and continue layering up in this way until all the ingredients have been used, ending with a layer of tomato sauce and Parmesan. Bake in a preheated oven at 200°C/400°F/Gas Mark 6 for 30 minutes. Serve hot, warm or cold, as preferred.

Serves 4
Preparation time: *40 minutes, plus 30 minutes draining*
Cooking time: *1 hour*
Oven temperature: *200°C/400°F/Gas Mark 6*

Spinach Tart
with ricotta and nutmeg

250 g/8 oz plain flour
pinch of salt
125 g/4 oz butter
1 egg yolk
2–3 tablespoons iced water

Filling
250 g/8 oz small tender spinach leaves
375 g/12 oz ricotta cheese
4 eggs, beaten
grated nutmeg
75 ml/3 fl oz single cream
25 g/1 oz grated Parmesan cheese
salt and freshly ground black pepper

sift the flour and salt into a mixing bowl and rub in the butter. Mix in the egg yolk and sufficient iced water to make a soft dough. Knead lightly until smooth. Leave in the refrigerator for at least 30 minutes to rest. Roll out the pastry to line a 25 cm/10 inch flan ring.

prick the base of the pastry case with a fork. Line it with a circle of baking paper, and half-fill with special ceramic baking beans or ordinary dried beans. Bake in a preheated oven at 200°C/400°F/Gas Mark 6 for 15 minutes.

remove the baking beans and paper and then return to the oven for a further 5 minutes to cook the base.

make the filling: cook the spinach in a little salted water for 3 minutes until softened but still a fresh bright green colour. Drain in a colander and squeeze out any excess water by pressing down hard with a plate. Chop the drained spinach.

put the ricotta in a bowl and beat in the chopped spinach, eggs, nutmeg, salt and pepper. Beat in the cream and continue beating until smooth. Spoon the filling into the pastry case and smooth the top.

sprinkle with Parmesan and bake at 180°C/350°F/Gas Mark 4 for 30 minutes until risen, set and golden brown.

Serves 8
Preparation time: *30 minutes, plus 30 minutes resting*
Cooking time: *30 minutes*
Oven temperature: *200°C/400°F/Gas Mark 6 then 180°C/350°F/Gas Mark 4*

Desserts and Baking

Sicilian Cheesecake

3 eggs, separated
125 g/4 oz caster sugar
finely grated rind of ½ lemon
125 g/4 oz plain flour
1 teaspoon baking powder

Filling

175 g/6 oz caster sugar
750 g/1½ lb ricotta cheese
⅛ teaspoon ground cinnamon
425g/14 oz mixed crystallized fruit, coarsely chopped
75 g/3 oz plain chocolate, chopped in small pieces
8 tablespoons Maraschino liqueur
extra cinnamon, to decorate

make the sponge: whisk the egg yolks with the sugar, lemon rind and 3 tablespoons of hot water until light and foamy. Sift the flour and baking powder together and fold it gently into the egg yolk mixture.

whisk the egg whites until they are stiff but not dry. Fold them into the sponge mixture. Pour the mixture into a buttered 25 cm/10 inch spring-form cake tin and bake in a preheated oven at 190°C/375°F/Gas Mark 5 for 15–20 minutes or until the cake is golden and springs back when pressed. Turn out and cool.

make the filling: dissolve the sugar in 3 tablespoons of water over low heat. Beat the syrup with the ricotta cheese until well blended. Beat the cinnamon into the ricotta mixture and put aside a few tablespoons for decoration. Stir 250 g/8 oz of the chopped fruit and chocolate into the rest of the mixture.

line the base of the cake tin with greaseproof paper. Cut the sponge in half horizontally and put one layer on the base, cut side up. Sprinkle with half of the Maraschino and spread with the ricotta mixture. Place the other sponge layer on top and sprinkle with the remaining Maraschino. Fit the ring of the tin in position and chill for several hours. To serve, remove from the tin, coat the top and sides with the reserved ricotta mixture and decorate with the reserved chopped fruit and a sprinkling of cinnamon. .

Serves 6–8
Preparation time: *40 minutes, plus 2–3 hours chilling*
Cooking time: *20–25 minutes*
Oven temperature: *190°C/375°F/Gas Mark 5*

Zabaglione

Simple ingredients produce this feather-light, foamy, whipped dessert. Make it immediately before serving, as it is liable to separate if left to stand for more than a few minutes.

4 eggs, separated
5 tablespoons caster sugar
8 tablespoons Marsala or sweet white wine

To serve
amaretti (almond macaroon biscuits)

separate the eggs and put the egg yolks in the top of a double boiler or in a basin sitting over a small saucepan of gently simmering water. Make sure that the basin is not in contact with the water below.

add the sugar and Marsala or sweet white wine to the egg yolks and mix together thoroughly..

beat the mixture with either a wire whisk or a hand-held electric whisk until the zabaglione is thick, light and hot. Even with an electric whisk, this will take 10–15 minutes, so be patient. Check that the water simmers gently underneath and does not boil dry.

when the zabaglione is cooked, pour it carefully into 4 tall glasses and serve immediately, with sponge fingers or amaretti. To serve it cold, continue beating the mixture off the heat until it has cooled down completely. Mix the cold zabaglione with raspberries or sliced strawberries or peaches, if liked.

Serves 4
Preparation time: *2–3 minutes*
Cooking time: *10–15 minutes*

Panettone

Traditionally a Christmas treat, this rich yeast cake from Milan is now eaten throughout the year. At Easter, it is made in the shape of a dove and called Columba.

50 g/2 oz caster sugar
25 g/1 oz fresh yeast
150 ml/¼ pint lukewarm water
3 egg yolks
pinch of salt
475 g/15 oz strong plain flour
125 g/4 oz butter, softened
50 g/2 oz sultanas
50 g/2 oz raisins
50 g/2 oz chopped mixed peel
25 g/1 oz butter, melted

stir 1 teaspoon of the sugar and all of the yeast into the lukewarm water. Leave to stand for about 10 minutes until frothy. Beat the egg yolks in a large bowl and stir in the yeast mixture, salt and remaining sugar. Beat in 250 g/8 oz of the flour and then gradually beat in the softened butter, a little at a time. Knead in the remaining flour to make a dough.

turn out the dough on to a lightly floured surface and knead well until the dough is firm and elastic. Place in a lightly oiled polythene bag and leave in a warm place until well risen and doubled in size.

turn out the dough on to a lightly floured surface and knead in the sultanas, raisins and peel. Continue kneading until the fruit is evenly distributed. Place the dough in a greased 18 cm/7 inch round cake tin and cover with some oiled clingfilm. Leave in a warm place until the dough rises to the top of the tin.

remove the clingfilm and brush the top of the dough with some of the melted butter. Bake in a preheated oven at 200°C/400°F/Gas Mark 6 for 20 minutes. Reduce the oven temperature to 180°C/350°F/Gas Mark 4 and cook for a further 20–30 minutes. Remove from the tin and brush the top and sides with the remaining melted butter. Serve warm or cold, cut into thin slices.

Serves 10
Preparation time: 1 1/2 hours
Cooking time: 40–50 minutes
Oven temperature: 200°C/400°F/Gas Mark 6 then 180°C/350°F/Gas Mark 4

Neapolitan Tart
with ricotta and almonds

The filling in this traditional latticed tart is rich and fruity, with a distinctive almond flavour.

250 g/8 oz plain flour
pinch of salt
125 g/4 oz butter
1 egg yolk
2–3 tablespoons iced water
icing sugar for dusting

Filling
375 g/12 oz ricotta cheese
75 g/3 oz caster sugar
3 eggs, well beaten
50 g/2 oz blanched almonds, finely chopped
50 g/2 oz chopped mixed peel
finely grated rind of ½ lemon
juice and finely grated rind of ½ orange
¼ teaspoon vanilla essence

sift the flour and salt into a mixing bowl and rub in the butter with the fingertips until the mixture resembles fine breadcrumbs. Mix in the egg yolk and add enough iced water to form a soft dough. Knead lightly and leave to chill in the refrigerator for 30 minutes. Roll out the pastry to line a 20 cm/8 inch flan ring. Reserve the pastry trimmings.

make the filling: rub the ricotta cheese through a sieve into a basin and then beat in the sugar. Gradually beat in the eggs and then add the almonds, peel, lemon and orange rind and juice and the vanilla essence, beating well between each addition.

pour the ricotta cheese filling into the prepared pastry case and then smooth over the surface.

roll out the reserved pastry trimmings and then using a fluted roller, cut into thin 1 cm/½ inch wide strips. Arrange them in a criss-cross pattern over the top of the flan. Bake in the centre of a preheated oven at 180°C/350°F/Gas Mark 4 for 45–50 minutes or until set and golden. Cool and serve cold, rather than chilled, dusted with icing sugar.

Serves 6–8
Preparation time: *20 minutes, plus 30 minutes chilling*
Cooking time: *45–50 minutes*
Oven temperature: *180°C/350°F/Gas Mark 4*

Caramelized Oranges

If you have plenty of oranges, and want to make a really pretty, fresh-tasting dessert, this is a simple and quickly made recipe.

12 oranges
175 g/6 oz sugar
125 ml/4 fl oz water

pare the rind thinly from one of the oranges and cut it into fine strips. Cook the strips in a small pan of boiling water for 2–3 minutes or until softened. Drain well and put aside.

remove and discard all the pith and peel from the oranges with a sharp knife. Put the oranges in a large heatproof bowl. Sprinkle the strips of orange rind over the top.

put the sugar and water in a saucepan and heat gently, stirring constantly, until the sugar dissolves completely. Bring to the boil and boil hard until the syrup changes to a rich golden caramel. Take care that the caramel does not become too dark as it will continue to cook after the pan is removed from the heat. If it is too thick, stand well back and add 2 tablespoons of hot water, then stir well.

pour the caramel over the oranges and set aside to cool. Put in the refrigerator and leave to chill overnight. To serve, transfer the oranges and caramel to an attractive serving dish and serve with whipped cream. Note: if wished, the oranges can be cut into thin slices horizontally, and secured with cocktail sticks before adding the caramel.

Serves 6
Preparation time: *15 minutes*
Cooking time: *8–10 minutes, plus chilling time*

Amaretto Soufflés
with almonds and vanilla

4 macaroons
75 ml/3 fl oz Amaretto di Saronno
150 ml/¼ pint milk
1 drop vanilla essence
15 g/½ oz butter
25 g/1 oz strong plain white flour
4 egg yolks (1 kept separately)
4 egg whites
25 g/1 oz caster sugar
sifted icing sugar to decorate

Almond purée
75 g/3 oz flaked almonds
150 ml/¼ pint milk
2 teaspoons sugar

make the almond purée: put the almonds, milk and sugar in a saucepan and bring to the boil.

reduce the heat and simmer gently for a few minutes. Cool slightly and then blend in a food processor or liquidizer until thoroughly mixed.

grease and flour 4 individual soufflé dishes, each 7.5 cm/3 inch in diameter. Soak the macaroons in half the Amaretto and put 1 macaroon, cut into quarters, in each prepared soufflé dish.

make the soufflé mixture: put two-thirds of the milk in a heavy-based saucepan with the vanilla and butter and bring to the boil. Remove from the heat and stir in the remaining milk with the flour and 1 egg yolk.

heat again until the mixture thickens and whisk briefly. Add the remaining egg yolks and cook for 2 minutes over low heat.

whisk the egg whites until stiff and then whisk in the sugar. Blend the soufflé mixture with the almond purée and the remaining Amaretto.

fold in the beaten egg whites carefully . Spoon this mixture into the soufflé dishes and cook in a preheated oven at 220°C/425°F/Gas Mark 7 for 10–12 minutes. Dust with icing sugar.

Serves 4
Preparation time: *25 minutes*
Cooking time: *15–20 minutes*
Oven temperature: *220°C/425°F/Gas Mark 7*

Sicilian Peach Water Ice

Sicilian fruit-based water ices taste wonderful. You can make them with other fruits such as melon, with excellent results.

125 g/4 oz sugar

150 ml/¼ pint water

4 large peaches or melon (see clipboard below)

juice of 1 lemon

put the sugar and water into a small pan and heat gently until the sugar has dissolved, then boil for 3–4 minutes. Leave until quite cold.

immerse the peaches in boiling water for 1 minute, then drain and remove the skins and stones. Immediately purée the flesh in an electric blender or press through a nylon sieve.

mix with the lemon juice to prevent discolouration. Stir in the cold syrup, pour into a shallow freezer tray and freeze until half firm.

turn into a bowl and whisk vigorously for a few minutes, then return to the tray and freeze until firm.

transfer to the refrigerator 30–40 minutes before serving to allow the ice to soften a little. To serve, scoop the water ice into individual glasses.

Serves 4
Preparation time: *15 minutes, plus freezing and 30–40 minutes chilling*

clipboard: Melon ice can be made the same way by replacing the peaches in this recipe with 750 g/1½ lb ripe, peeled and deseeded Charentais or Ogen melon flesh.

Almond Peaches
with amaretti filling

*These almond-flavoured baked peaches are a speciality
of the Piedmont region in the north of Italy.*

4 large firm peaches, halved and pitted
75 g/3 oz amaretti, crushed (see clipboard below)
50 g/2 oz caster sugar
40 g/1½ oz butter, softened
1 egg yolk
½ teaspoon finely grated lemon rind

scoop a little flesh from the centre of each peach half and put in a basin.

add the amaretti crumbs, sugar, 25 g/1 oz of the butter, the egg yolk and lemon rind and beat until smooth.

divide between the peaches, shaping the stuffing into a mound. Top with flaked almonds if liked, and dot with the remaining butter.

arrange in a buttered ovenproof dish. Bake in a preheated moderate oven at 180°C/350°F/Gas Mark 4 for 25–35 minutes. Serve warm or cold with pouring cream.

Serves 4
Preparation time: *20 minutes*
Cooking time: *25–35 minutes*
Oven temperature: *180°C/350°F/Gas Mark 4*

Clipboard: Amaretti biscuits are very popular in Italy. They have a distinctive almond flavour, and are typical accompaniments to Italian desserts. They are now widely available in large supermarkets, as well as in Italian food shops.

Ricotta Bombe
with rum

Ricotta, the soft cheese made from ewe's milk features in a multitude of Italian recipes. Here it is used to make a creamy, ice-cold dessert, a speciality of the countryside around Rome.

5 egg yolks
125 g/4 oz caster sugar
5 tablespoons rum
500 g/1 lb fresh ricotta cheese, sieved

line a 1.2 litre/2 pint freezerproof mould with kitchen foil.

put the egg yolks and sugar in a bowl, and whisk with an electric or hand whisk until light and fluffy.

fold in the rum until it is thoroughly amalgamated, then fold in the ricotta a little at a time.

spoon the mixture into the prepared mould, smooth the surface, then cover with kitchen foil.

freeze until solid. Unmould on to a serving plate and serve immediately with Amaretti or brandysnaps.

Serves 4–6
Preparation time: *20 minutes, plus freezing*

Tiramisu
Mascarpone Coffee Dessert

Mascarpone cheese is almost as rich as clotted cream, and Tiramisu is one of the most popular dessert recipes featuring it. If you like, you can decorate the top with grated chocolate.

2 egg yolks

2 tablespoons caster sugar

few drops vanilla essence

250 g/8 oz mascarpone cheese

175 ml/6 fl oz strong black coffee

2 tablespoons Marsala

1 tablespoon brandy

150 g/5 oz sponge fingers

1 tablespoon cocoa powder

2 tablespoons grated dark chocolate (optional)

mix together the egg yolks and sugar in a bowl, beating with a wooden spoon until they are creamy. Add the vanilla essence and fold in the mascarpone. The mixture should be thick and creamy.

make the strong black coffee in a jug or cafetière, then mix with the Marsala and brandy in a bowl. Quickly dip the sponge fingers in the coffee mixture. They should absorb just enough liquid to flavour them without going soggy and falling apart.

arrange some of the soaked sponge fingers in the base of a large attractive glass serving bowl or 4 individual serving dishes. Cover with a layer of the mascarpone mixture.

continue layering alternate layers of sponge fingers and mascarpone, finished with a top layer of mascarpone. Sift the cocoa over the top, then chill in the refrigerator for 3–4 hours or until set. The flavour improves if the coffee dessert is left overnight.

Serves 6
Preparation time: *20 minutes, plus 3–4 hours chilling*

Breads

Panini

Grissini

Panettone

Pandoro

Baguette

Pandoro
Pandoro is a tall, shaped yeast cake which is very similar to panettone but is made without the fruit. It is served for breakfast with coffee and also on special occasions such as Christmas and Easter.

Panini
Panini simply means 'little bread' and is a typical Italian table bread, baked in the form of a small, flat, loaf. Like all all Italian bread, panini is made with yeast. It is made fresh every day, and served with all meals.

Baguette
The baguette is traditionally associated with France. Originally from Paris, it is a long, thin crusty loaf made with white flour, and it is delicious eaten with cheese. It is an international bread, baked all over the world.

Panettone
Panettone is a yeast cake made with egg yolk and candied fruit. Made in the shape of a tall loaf, it is a speciality of Northern Italy. It is very popular in Europe, and is served for breakfast and special occasions.

Focaccia

Ciabatta

Grissini
Every Italian restaurant worth its salt has welcoming stacks of delicious, crunchy Grissini on the table. It is a long, thin, crisp dry bread which is pale gold in colour and is served as an appetiser.

Focaccia
Foccacia is a flat, Italian yeast bread, made with olive oil as a key ingredient and baked in an oiled pan. It is often flavoured with garlic. Focaccia is served with different toppings such as sun-dried tomatoes, olives or fresh herbs. It is equally delicious eaten by itself or with a filling.

Ciabatta
Ciabatta is one of the most popular of all Italian breads. Like foccacia it is made with olive oil, and baked into a fairly flat loaf with a distinctive open texture. Ciabatta can be cooked with a delicious range of flavourings such as sun-dried tomatoes, olives and herbs.

Garlic Focaccia

Panne all'olio, *Italian olive oil bread has become universally popular. It is healthy and delicious, and not at all difficult to make —* try this garlic-flavoured version.

5 g/¼ oz dry yeast
1 teaspoon sugar
375 g/12 oz plain flour
175 ml/6 fl oz lukewarm water
1 teaspoon salt
3 cloves garlic, crushed
2 tablespoons olive oil
1 tablespoon maize flour or semolina
1 tablespoon olive oil, plus extra for glazing
2 teaspoons finely crushed sea salt

combine the yeast, sugar, 1 teaspoon flour and water in a small mixing bowl. Stand, covered with clingfilm, in a warm place for 10 minutes or until foamy.

sift the remaining flour and salt into a large mixing bowl. Add garlic and stir with a knife to combine. Make a well in the centre, stir in the yeast mixture and olive oil. Using a flat-bladed knife, mix to a firm dough.

turn out the dough on to lightly floured surface, and knead for 10 minutes. Shape the dough into a ball, and place in a large, lightly oiled mixing bowl. Stand, covered with clingfilm, in a warm place for 40 minutes or until well risen.

preheat oven to moderately hot, 210°C/415°F/Gas Mark 6–7. Sprinkle the base of an 18 x 28 cm/7 x 11 inch shallow baking tin with maize flour or semolina. Knead the dough again for 2 minutes or until smooth. Press dough into the tin, and prick deep holes with a skewer.

sprinkle lightly with water and place in the oven. Bake for 10 minutes and sprinkle again with water. Bake for a further 10 minutes, brush with extra olive oil, sprinkle with sea salt, then bake for 5 more minutes. Serve warm or at room temperature, cut into squares.

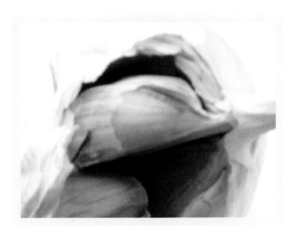

Serves 4–6
Preparation time: *20 minutes, plus 50 minutes standing*
Cooking time: *25 minutes*
Oven temperature: *210°C/415°F/Gas Mark 6–7*

Cheese Focaccia
with fresh chives

Cheese and chives complement each other well,
and give a robust flavour to the focaccia.

5 g/¼ oz dry yeast
1 teaspoon sugar
375 g/12 oz plain flour
175 ml/6 fl oz lukewarm water
1 teaspoon salt
25 g/1 oz Parmesan cheese, finely grated
1 tablespoon finely chopped chives
2 tablespoons olive oil
1 tablespoon maize flour or semolina
1 tablespoon olive oil plus
extra for glazing
2 teaspoons finely crushed sea salt

combine the yeast, sugar, 1 teaspoon flour and water in small mixing bowl. Stand, covered with clingfilm, in a warm place for 10 minutes or until foamy.

sift the remaining flour and salt into a large mixing bowl. Add Parmesan and chives, and stir with a knife to combine. Make a well in the centre, stir in the yeast mixture and olive oil. Mix to a firm dough with a knife.

turn out the dough on to lightly floured surface, and knead for 10 minutes. Shape the dough into a ball, and place in a large, lightly oiled mixing bowl. Stand, covered with clingfilm, in a warm place for 40 minutes or until well risen.

preheat oven to moderately hot, 210°C/415°F/Gas Mark 6 – 7). Sprinkle the base of an 18 x 28 cm/7 x 11 inch shallow tin with maize flour or semolina. Knead the dough again for 2 minutes or until smooth. Press dough into the tin; prick deep holes with a skewer. Sprinkle lightly with water and place in the oven. Bake for 10 minutes and sprinkle again with water. Bake for a further 10 minutes, brush with the extra olive oil, sprinkle with sea salt, then bake for 5 more minutes. Serve warm or at room temperature, cut into squares.

Serves 4–6
Preparation time: *20 minutes, plus 50 minutes standing*
Cooking time: *25 minutes*
Oven temperature: *210°C/415°F/Gas Mark 6–7*

Olive Focaccia
with rosemary and garlic

5 g/¼ oz dry yeast
1 teaspoon sugar
375 g/12 oz plain flour
175 ml/6 fl oz lukewarm water
1 teaspoon salt
1 clove garlic, crushed
2 tablespoons olive oi
50–75 g/2–3 oz pitted black olives, finely chopped
1 tablespoon fresh rosemary leaves
1 tablespoon maize flour or semolina
1 tablespoon olive oil, plus extra for glazing
2 teaspoons finely crushed sea salt

To garnish
few whole black olives
few sprigs fresh rosemary

combine the yeast, sugar, 1 teaspoon flour and water in a small mixing bowl. Stand, covered with clingfilm, in a warm place for 10 minutes or until foamy.

sift the remaining flour and salt into a large mixing bowl. Add the garlic, olives and rosemary and stir with a knife to combine. Make a well in the centre, stir in the yeast mixture and olive oil. Using a flat-bladed knife, mix to a firm dough.

turn out the dough on to lightly floured surface, and knead for 10 minutes. Shape the dough into a ball, and place in a large, lightly oiled mixing bowl. Stand, covered with clingfilm, in a warm place for 40 minutes or until well risen.

preheat oven to moderately hot, 210°C/415°F/Gas Mark 6–7. Sprinkle the base of an 18 x 28 cm/7 x 11 inch shallow baking tin with maize flour or semolina. Knead the dough again for 2 minutes or until smooth. Press dough into the tin, and prick deep holes with a skewer.

sprinkle lightly with water and place in the oven. Bake for 10 minutes and sprinkle again with water. Bake for a further 10 minutes, brush with extra olive oil, sprinkle with sea salt, then bake for 5 more minutes. Serve warm or at room temperature, cut into squares.

Serves: 4–6
Preparation time: *15 minutes*
Cooking time: *45 minutes*
Oven temperature: *210°C/415°F/Gas Mark 6–7*

Index

Acknowledgments

Photo Credits
Jean Cazals: front cover, back cover

Special photography by Jean Cazals

All other photos:
Octopus Publishing Group Ltd. / William Adams-Lingwood,
Robert Golden, Tim Imrie, Graham Kirk, James Murphy,
Peter Myers, Simon Smith, Roger Stowell, Paul Webster,
Paul Williams.

Home economist
Marie-Ange Lapierre